## The Search for Lost Worlds

James Wellard has written extensively on North Africa and the Sahara. A distinguished novelist and journalist, he was a war correspondent from 1941 to 1945, and subsequently a foreign correspondent. His other books include *The Great Sahara*, a history of exploration in the desert, and *Lost Worlds of Africa*, the record of his own travels.

# The Search for Lost Worlds

An exploration of the lands of myth and legend,
including Atlantis, Sheba and Avalon

**James Wellard**

**A Pan Original**
Pan Books Ltd  London and Sydney

### Acknowledgements

We are grateful to the following for the illustrations, and for permission to use copyright prints and photographs: Ian Fleming & Associates; Mary Evans Picture Library, 9; Mansell Collection, 1, 2, 3, 6, 7, 8, 11; University Library, Heidelberg, 10.

First published 1975 by Pan Books Ltd,
Cavaye Place, London sw10 9pg
ISBN 0 330 24253 9
© James Wellard 1975

Printed in Great Britain by
Hazell Watson & Viney Ltd, Aylesbury, Bucks

# Contents

## Part Three
### Lost Lands of the British Isles

# *Foreword*

THERE are literally thousands of books and articles on the subject of the lost worlds of antiquity, and there will undoubtedly be thousands more, for men have always been intrigued by legends of places which have disappeared from the map, and they will always go on searching for them. There are, as we shall see, a great many of these vanished utopias, the more interesting of which will be discussed in this survey.

The story of Atlantis, of Lemuria, Mu, the Garden of Eden, Arcadia, the Isles of the Blest, the country of the Amazons, of the Queen of Sheba, and other undiscovered places is perennially fresh and fascinating. One reason is that the more technically advanced our society becomes, and the greater the conformity that results from mechanization, the more we tend to look back nostalgically to those Golden Ages which the legends of almost every nation recall in their folk literature, legends which often tell us of islands and whole continents that have sunk below the seas at the dawn of human history.

There is also another reason for the continual inter-

est in the Atlantis-type myth: namely, the excitement
engendered by the search itself. For the disappearance
of entire civilizations or communities and the whereabouts of the lost island-continents constitutes a mystery which involves the hunting down and sifting of
all kinds of evidence, very much as the detective has to
hunt down clues in order to solve a crime.

This survey of the enormous literature of some of
the more significant of the lost worlds, then, is intended to set out the evidence whereby the reader can
decide for himself what theories are credible and what
are unacceptable on one ground or another. In doing
so, he will discover in an extraordinary manner the
eccentricities as well as the scholarship of some of those
who have attempted to solve the mystery. For, in general, there are two approaches to the problem of historical or legendary lost worlds; one, the scientific
approach in which the only evidence seriously considered is factual, or at least logical; and the other, a
mystical attitude in which the evidence is largely
derived from the writer's imagination.

And so it will be seen that the Atlantis myth in its
multifarious forms, beginning with the Sumerian
saga called the *Epic of Gilgamesh* dating from 2,000
BC and re-appearing throughout recorded history right
up to our own era, has meant almost all things to all
men, sometimes an historical reality and sometimes a
private dream. Thus, to a philosopher like Plato, the
story of a civilization that disappeared beneath the Atlantic was not only an actual episode, but an event of
profound moral significance. To a scientist like Aris-

totle, on the other hand, it was merely a poetic fantasy. To later Greek and Roman geographers, it was a mystery beyond solution since their precise knowledge of the world was virtually restricted to the confines of southern and western Europe; while the scholars of the medieval world were more interested in theological than in geophysical problems.

Only after the discovery of the Americas did the historians and geographers start anew the search for the lost lands, for the existence of a continent which Plato actually hinted at and no westerner had yet seen stimulated both the professional and amateur scholars to now look beneath and beyond the Atlantic Ocean. By the end of the 19th century, a mass of evidence had been accumulated from the fields of history, geography, geology, and mythology, and Atlantis itself had been located in almost every corner of the globe, from Sweden in the north to Nigeria in the south, and from Japan in the east to the Pacific in the west.

And in addition to searching for Atlantis, students of history and mythology turned their attention to other vanished places made famous in legend – the Gardens of the Hesperides, the Cassiterides, the Garden of Eden, the Isles of the Blest, Avalon, Lyonnesse, and so forth. In fact, the visionaries in particular now proceeded to discover still more unknown continents, which they named Lemuria, Mu, and Uranus, frequently supporting their claims by references to mysterious documents hidden in Phoenician vases or written in indecipherable languages or acquired by communion with the spirit world.

One result of all this speculation based on spurious evidence and inconclusive 'proof' was that Atlantology, as the study of lost lands came to be called, fell into disrepute among professional scholars and was dismissed by almost all of them as a sort of playground for cranks. The term 'Atlantomaniacs' was invented to define those students of the subject whose enthusiasm ran away with them, just as the expression 'Etruscomaniacs' was given to those amateur linguists who claimed to have deciphered a language which continues to baffle the world's leading philologists.

The reader, then, will meet with many curious ideas in the following pages, and it will be up to him to decide whether, for instance, the Atlanteans were the blue-eyed, vegetarian, teetotal ancestors of the Aryan race, as a German Atlantologist maintains; or whether they were twenty-seven feet high 'with bodies of a hardness sufficient to bend a steel bar,' as one of the mystical school declares.

In contrast, and by way of restoring respectability, as it were, to the controversy, the field has been methodically explored during the last decades by a team of professional archaeologists, with some impressive results which have been reported at some length in Chapter Four.

In brief, as much of the evidence as it is possible to give in this short survey of the enormous literature of the subject has been presented so that the reader can assess both the facts and the fictions. And whereas his final impression may be that there is little more to be said on the subject of such lost island-continents as

Atlantis, Lemuria, and Mu, he may still be stimulated to follow up what clues we have in the old Celtic myths of submerged lands variously called Lyonnesse, Ys, Mayda, and others. If so, it is hoped that the bibliography provided at the end of this book will provide the basis for further research.

It remains to thank the Superintendent and staff of the British Museum Reading Room for making available the books and facilities for the writing of this survey, with acknowledgements to the generations of Atlantologists who go back at least as far as Plato, the first narrator of the exciting story of a lost world. The relevant passages of the Greek philosopher's description are given in the Appendix.

# Part One

## *Lost Lands of the Atlantic and Pacific Oceans*

### 1: PLATO'S ATLANTIS

THOUSANDS of years ago, long before men had invented writing and were able to keep permanent records, some tremendous cataclysm overwhelmed those regions of the world where western civilization began. This unparalleled disaster lingered on in the folk-memory of all the peoples of the eastern Mediterranean, and, in time, was recorded in quasi-mythological form in the literature of the Sumerians, the Hebrews, the Greeks, and the Egyptians. While all these epics vary in minor details, they all agree on the nature and extent of the catastrophe: the world, as they knew it, was torn apart by violent convulsions, consumed by fire, and submerged beneath rising floods of water. There can be no doubt now that the Sumerian Epic of Gilgamesh and the account in the seventh chapter of Genesis describe the same Deluge which almost wiped out life in Mesopotamia; while the Greek myth of Deucalion and his ark was derived from a story passed down through many generations of a similar, if not the same, cataclysm.

The Egyptians, too, had their memories of some terrible calamity, and from their records comes the strange story of a large, prosperous, and highly civilized island-kingdom which disappeared beneath the Atlantic Ocean in a single day and night of indescribable terror and destruction.

The world first heard of this catastrophe in about 350 BC when it was described by Plato in two of his later Dialogues, *Timaeus* and *Critias*. The story was so sensational that it was dismissed as fiction by, for instance, no less an authority than Aristotle, though it was just as vehemently defended as historical fact by the eminent Greek academician Crantor. The argument has been raging ever since and is as keen today as it was 2,300 years ago.

Atlantis, in fact, has become the symbolic personification of all the lost worlds and all the utopias that men have either sought or dreamt of, and it attracts into its orbit the legends of many other secret places which some maintain are mere myths, others the folk-memories of actual countries which have vanished from the face of the globe.

It has led, too, to the creation of whole new philosophies and sciences, particularly in the sphere of mysticism. Theosophy, anthroposophy, spiritualism, astral clairvoyance – these are some of the occult doctrines which have drawn deeply on the Atlantis myth for their inspiration.

Literally tens of thousands of books and articles have been written on the subject and will no doubt continue to be written. Atlantean societies have been formed in many parts of the world, and their journals issued to subscribers always eager for new facts, theories, or speculation. The epitome of what has been called Atlantomania was reached with the creation by the Danes in the twenties of a Principality of Atlantis, nominating the then Prince Christian as president and boasting its own flag, national anthem, and postage stamps.

In brief, the subject has intrigued and amused men since Plato first told the story of the rise and fall of an empire which flourished far to the west, somewhere beyond the Pillars of Hercules in the Atlantic Ocean. According to Plato, then, civilization was not only far older than men had dreamt of, but its origins were not confined to the peoples of the eastern Mediterranean. This is the essential significance of the story of Atlantis.

It is only fair to say that probably the account of the disappearance of a great empire beneath the waves would never have been taken very seriously if it had not been vouched for by the greatest philosopher of all time, and vouched for not as a myth or an allegory, but as historical fact. Plato is quite clear on that point.

And because of the great philosopher's assurances, men have continually sought for his lost kingdom, and, indeed, many have been convinced that they have found it – in Peru, the West Indies, the Canary Islands, Nigeria, Morocco, the Central Sahara, Tunisia, Spanish Andalusia, the English Channel, Heligoland, Sweden, Cyprus, Crete, Palestine, and Ceylon. It was the conviction that Atlantis, like the Etruscan language, had become 'the playground of cranks' that led

Dr Jowett, Plato's greatest English translator, to make such pronouncements as 'it was a legend so adapted to the human mind that it made a habitation for itself in any country. It was an island in the clouds, which might be seen anywhere by the eye of faith. . . . No one knew better than Plato how to invent a noble lie.'[1]

The contrary, of course, is the case. Plato gave the story to the world as a factual account of a recorded historical event, though his later commentators, for various reasons which we shall discuss in this book, have never ceased to argue about its authenticity. This uncertainty is partly responsible for the perennial fascination of Atlantis, for we can all read Plato's report and ask ourselves whether it is fact or fiction, or whether it is worth wondering about at all. And once this process of detection begins, Atlantis can become a part-time hobby or even a lifetime's research.

Those, of course, who state point-blank that Atlantis was a figment of Plato's imagination, a myth woven into one of his characteristic dialogues between Socrates and a disciple called Critias, do not need to look farther for evidence of this lost world submerged beneath the Atlantic or some other ocean. We have noted that Plato's younger contemporary Aristotle, for instance, flatly rejected the existence of any such place, which greatly impressed his followers right up through the Middle Ages, but which really shows how dogmatic this great scientist was. For just as he was totally wrong in his astronomical doctrines, so he could have been wrong in his dismissal of Atlantis as a geographical feature of pre-Hellenic history.

On the whole, the majority of learned students tend to agree with Aristotle on the grounds that Plato's story contains many obvious inconsistencies; and they became even more sceptical of the whole affair as amateur historians and self-appointed mystics proposed more and more outlandish solutions to the problem.

Be that as it may, the arguments for or against believing that Atlantis was once an actual place on the map must come from the internal evidence within the story itself, which we will now give in summary form before going on to discuss the theories arising from it.

I will tell you a story, Socrates (Plato begins), which is extraordinary but absolutely true.

The speaker is a young man called Critias who goes on to say that he heard it from his grandfather who heard it, in turn, from his father, a kinsman and friend of none other than Solon, the father of Greek law.

Solon, it appears, had visited the Egyptian city of Sais on the Nile delta soon after 600 BC. His work of framing a constitution for Athens and of instituting social and economic reforms was ended, and he had decided to devote the remaining years of his life to writing history and poetry – intending to combine the two arts into one, in the manner of Homer. And so while in Sais, which had close associations with Greece through trade and colonization, Solon consulted the Egyptian scholars and their archives as to the origins of the Hellenic civilization, stressing the point that he was more interested in facts than fables which at that time formed the basis of his nation's pre-history.

The Egyptian priests then told him that whereas
the early records of most nations had been destroyed
by fires, floods, and wars, those of Egypt had been preserved: first, because the Nile Valley was relatively
safe from natural cataclysms; and secondly, because
the records were cut in stone and housed in the temples.

One of these records told of events which took place
9,000 years before and which particularly concerned
the Greeks and the city of Athens which in those days
excelled all others in virtue and wisdom. Many great
and wonderful deeds had been performed by the
Athenians, said the priests, but one of them exceeded
all the others in greatness and valour; and that was the
defeat of a mighty power which had suddenly come out
of the west with its invincible armies and had begun
conquering most of Europe and Asia.

The invaders came from an island situated beyond
the straits which geographers call the Pillars of Hercules. This island was larger than Libya and Asia put
together and was the stepping-stone, as it were, to other
islands which stretched across the Atlantic Ocean to
another continent. The name of this country from
which the invasion of Europe came was Atlantis, or,
in its Greek form, the Island of Atlas.

Now this island and its people were highly civilized
and had already colonized the adjacent islands as well
as parts of the continents on either side of the Ocean.
In fact, armies from Atlantis had invaded North Africa
and conquered it up to the frontiers of Egypt; and on
the other side of the Mediterranean Atlantean batta-
lions had marched across southern Europe as far as the

Greek borders. At this juncture the invaders decided to conquer both Egypt and Greece and thus make themselves masters of the known world. In the meantime, all the other invaded countries had given up the struggle, leaving Athens to stand alone against this mighty power. Indeed, the Athenians were almost brought to their knees, but finally defeated and drove the Atlanteans back – drove them right across Europe and Africa back to their island homeland. Athens had saved the Mediterranean world from slavery.

But soon after this victory, a terrible cataclysm occurred, with violent earthquakes and floods. In fact, in a single day and night of rain, the Athenian forces were washed away and the island of Atlas sank back beneath the sea and vanished never to be seen again. And this is the reason why the sea in the area where Atlantis existed is so shallow due to the subsidence of the land.

What sort of country was this kingdom which existed beyond the Pillars of Hercules? And why was it powerful enough to conquer most of Africa and Europe?

Plato gives the answers to these questions in another of his philosophical essays in which that same Critias who told the story of Solon's visit to Egypt in the dialogue entitled *Timaeus* gives further details concerning the lost island. These details are of paramount importance to researchers who seek to prove the authenticity of Atlantis, whereas to those who suspect that the whole concept of an empire somewhere in the Atlantic Ocean was merely a figment of Plato's imagination. Critias's description reads like pure fiction. At all events, this is what we are told.

Atlantis was the island of Poseidon: that is, it was under the protection of the sea-god, who according to myth populated it by his union with a mortal woman called Cleito. The islanders became exceedingly rich and prosperous, for their country was practically self sufficient: it not only provided them with the necessities of life, but was rich in precious metals, notably orichalc and gold. Students have never been able to agree on what the metal orichalc (Greek ὀρείχαλκος) is supposed to be, for its literal meaning is 'mountain copper'. Plato says that it 'glowed like fire'; and since he states that orichalc was the most valuable of all metals except gold, perhaps he is referring to brass, an alloy of copper and zinc which was far rarer in the ancient world than bronze, the alloy of copper and tin. In fact, brass which contains about eighty per cent of copper can 'glow like fire' and, of course, resembles gold.

In addition to the mineral resources the island of Atlantis was rich in forests which provided timber for houses and the fleets of ships which carried on a profitable trade with the outside world. The country abounded in wild animals, including elephants, and every kind of vegetable flourished in the rich soil, besides 'fruits having a hard rind, affording drinks and meats and ointments, and a good supply of chestnuts and the like, and the pleasant kind of dessert which consoles us after dinner when we are full and tired of eating'.

This island 'lying beneath the sun' was famous for its temples and palaces and harbours and docks. The description of the principal palace as given in *Critias* supplies the main clue to what many students consider the most convincing explanation of this curious Platonic myth. The palace, says the record, was built over the original habitation of Poseidon when he visited the island, and every new king tried to surpass his predecessors in making the building a marvel for size and beauty. Eventually it consisted of a series of residences conjoined in a great complex of stone buildings whose walls were bright with colours. In the centre was the holy temple dedicated to Cleito and Poseidon, a place absolutely forbidden to all but the king and his priests, for it was on this spot that the sea-god begat the royal dynasty on a mortal woman. And within this sanctuary sacred bulls were allowed to roam about. Hither came the ten kings of Atlantis for their quinquennial conferences at which they debated national affairs, pledged themselves to uphold the law, and passed judgment on those who had broken it.

There follows an extraordinary description of the ritual which took place in this 'bull-palace':

There were bulls who had the range of the temple of Poseidon; and the ten kings who were left alone in the temple, after they had offered prayers to the gods that they might take the sacrifices which were acceptable to them, hunted the bulls, without weapons, but with staves and nooses; and the bull which they caught they led up to the column; the victim was then struck on the head by them and slain over the sacred inscription. . . . After they had eaten, when darkness came on, and the fire about the sacrifice was cool, all of them put on most beautiful azure robes and sitting on the ground, at night, near the embers of the sacrifices on which they had sworn, and extinguishing all the fire about the temple, they received and gave judgment.[1]

There is surely a description here, based on some kind of detailed records, of the palace of Minos, the Cretan king who was said to have been the offspring of Zeus disguised as a bull and Europa; who prayed to Poseidon to send him a bull from the sea for him to sacrifice; and who made war on Athens. All of these matters will be considered later in the discussion of the whereabouts of Atlantis.

The temple of Poseidon, says Plato, was noted for 'a sort of barbaric splendour' and for the statue of a charioteer with six winged horses and around him a frieze of a hundred nereids riding on dolphins.

The living apartments of the palace were provided with baths, both hot and cold, open and enclosed – baths for the king, his attendants, the queen, the women of the palace, and even the horses and cattle. The vast complex of royal residences was protected by a wall and guarded by special troops. Beyond the palace wall lay the beautiful countryside with mountains, rivers, lakes, and meadows all leading down to the sea coast. The coast had a number of large harbours and ports constantly busy with merchant vessels arriving and departing, discharging cargo and passengers day and night. The prosperity of the island and the happiness of its inhabitants were exceptional and continued to be so as long as they were obedient to the laws of god, prizing virtue above everything else, including material possessions. But once they became greedy and avaricious, they began to lose that love of virtue and wisdom which was the divine part of their nature inherited from their original progenitor Poseidon. They were no longer so gentle towards each other or so just in their relations with foreign powers. In short, they began to oppress their own people and to enslave those of other countries, conquering all of North Africa up to Egypt and Europe up to Greece.

It was at this stage of history, 9,000 years before Solon's visit to Egypt about 570 BC, that the Athenians became the saviours of Europe by driving back the vast armies of Atlanteans. They drove them back to the Pillars of Hercules, liberating all those nations overrun by the invaders. What would have happened after this great land victory of Athens over Atlantis will never be known, because at this critical moment in time a series of earthquakes and floods swallowed up the entire Greek army in one terrible day and night. It was this cataclysm, unparalleled in recorded history, that caused Atlantis to sink right into the sea and vanish for ever — its cities, temples, harbours, forests, mountains, and plains. Nothing remained to remind men that there was once such a mighty nation beyond the Pillars of Hercules, the only physical trace of its existence being those shoals and banks which navigators in those Atlantic waters where once the island rose out of the sea are careful to avoid.

This, then, is a summary of the Atlantis story as it is

found in two of Plato's dialogues, *Timaeus* and *Critias*.
So the detective work which needs to be done to discover whether the lost world described by the Greek
philosopher is myth or reality must start with the
*dramatis personae*, the people involved in the telling
of the story.

There are a half-a-dozen key characters. First, Plato,
the chief disciple of his beloved master Socrates: it was
Plato who recorded the famous dialogues which took
place sometimes in the market place, sometimes in
wooded groves outside the city during the glorious
5th century BC. He reports for us the editorial comments, as it were, made by Socrates himself, who, as a
lifelong seeker after truth, obviously wanted to know
the source of this extraordinary story. According to
Plato, Socrates's comment was: 'Does not your narrative, Critias, have the very great advantage of being
fact and not fiction? How and where else shall we find
another if we abandon this?'

The philosopher's response has puzzled students
ever since, for are we to take it at its face value, as the
considered opinion of a very shrewd observer of life; or
are the words faintly ironic – the kind of thing a wise
old man could say to a rather impetuous young one?

This consideration leads us to the character of Critias who together with two other young aristocrats,
Timaeus and Hermocrates, was a guest of Socrates,
Critias obviously knew of and respected his host's in-
sistence on truth, and so he prefaces his account of
Atlantis with certain facts which he brings forward as
evidence that his tale 'though strange, is certainly

true'. Socrates, no doubt, inquired how he could be sure any tale was true. Because it was vouched for by none other than Solon, the greatest of our lawgivers, Critias replied and, he added that Solon himself told it to my great-grandfather, Dropides, whose relative and very dear friend he was. Moreover, 'my grandfather had the original papers of Solon, and these papers are still in my possession'.

And how controversial this remark has become! For those who believe in Atlantis maintain that there would have been absolutely no point in Plato's giving these factual details unless Critias was telling a story that was, as he says, 'strange but certainly true'. In other words, why bring in a revered Greek hero like Solon, a great-grandfather Dropides, also celebrated in Athens, and the existence of an actual manuscript still in Critias's possession, a fact that Plato could have corroborated since the two men were related?

Conversely, those who reject the reality of Atlantis, Dr Jowett among them, reply that all these details are merely a literary device to whet the appetite of the audience, a device which has been used a thousand times or more since Plato's time and was effectively used in the same form in Pierre Benoît's famous novel *L'Atlantide* in which the location of Atlantis in the middle of the Sahara was recorded in the papers of a young Spahi lieutenant.

Moreover, says the sceptics, this same Critias who claims to have the original manuscript of Solon containing his notes taken at the time of his visit to the Egyptian priests declares in another place that he had spent the night ransacking his memory for details of the story his grandfather who was ninety had told him as a little boy of ten. There is no mention here of the notes with which, one assumes, Critias could have refreshed his memory.

Still another theory suggests that while Solon actually did hear some such story from the Egyptians, the priests were simply falling back on the folk memory of some ancient invasion, like that of the mysterious Sea People who, around the 13th century BC, first destroyed the Mycenaean civilization and then attacked Egypt with seaborne invasions. Such a theory is all the more credible in view of the difficulties of preserving national archives in those violent times when one invading force after another swept down from the north and east onto the urbanized communities of the eastern Mediterranean. Certainly we know from Egyptian monuments that there were such invaders as the 'Sea People', late Bronze Age warriors, who were finally stopped in their sweep through the civilized world not by Athens but by Ramses III (c. 1195–1164 BC). It is most tempting, therefore, to see the origin of the Atlantis myth in the legends of both Greeks and Egyptians who had reason to remember and pass down the tale of those unidentified people who appeared out of nowhere in their chariots and crossed the sea in their ships, a people with weapons made from an obviously superior metal, the *orichalc* of Atlantis, or the hard bronze which 'shone like fire'. And then, as a compliment to the internationally famed and respected Athenian Solon, did not the Egyptian priests, while showing their guest a stele in which Ramses III's victory over the Sea People was recorded in hieroglyphics, assure him that the Greeks, too, fought the invaders and to them should go a share of the honour and glory for the defeat of the Atlanteans?

But the solution of the mystery is not as simple as that.

At least, it did not seem so to other philosophers and historians of the classical world. Herodotus does not mention it at all, though he has heard of a people he calls the Atlantes who occupied the interior of Libya. Aristotle, as we have seen, dismissed the tale as a mere fable. Yet other equally learned men like Crantor accepted Plato's account as authentic on the grounds that friends of his had seen the columns on which the event was recorded in hieroglyphs. (*En passant,* one wonders whether there were any Greeks at this time who could read the original and whether the contemporary Egyptian dragomen resembled those guides today in their eagerness to tell visitors what they want to hear.) Still, other writers vouch for the existence of the Egyptian columns, including an obscure geographer called Marcellus who made a collection of travellers' reports which located seven islands in the Atlantic, one of which was sacred to Poseidon, whose inhabitants preserved from their ancestors the memory of an exceedingly large kingdom called Atlantis which had ruled over all the other islands in the Atlantic Ocean.

When we come to examine the comments of later and better informed geographers and historians, we find on the whole a certain reluctance on the part of these

scholars to commit themselves. No doubt the reason
is that by the first century of the Christian era, the
known world was far greater than it had been in Plato's
time; the Atlantic, once thought unfit for navigation,
had been opened up; new lands had been discovered;
and the old maps completely re-drawn. Consequently
some of the most learned men of their time like Posi-
donius, the tutor of Cicero, Strabo, one of the greatest
of classical geographers, and Pliny the historian are
very careful to avoid being dogmatic on the subject of
Atlantis. Their view was that the factual evidence for
its existence, on the one hand, was admittedly slim;
yet, on the other, that violent geophysical cataclysms
which had taken place through the millennia and, for
that matter, were still taking place, made it quite possible that whole islands could sink overnight beneath
the sea.

From the end of the classical period and through the
Middle Ages, Atlantis tended to be forgotten, or to
become identified with the utopias in which mystics
and humanists like Sir Thomas More were far more
interested. Two great events in modern history re-
newed interest in this lost world – the Revival of
Learning and the discovery of a new continent. For
Plato had definitely said in the *Timaeus* that there was
a continent on the western side of the Atlantic sea, 'for
this sea within the Straits of Hercules [i.e. of Gibraltar]
is only a harbour, having a narrow entrance, but that
other is a real sea, and the surrounding land may most
truly be called a continent'. Columbus had reached
that continent in 1497. His great voyage seemed to

prove, if not the full authenticity of Plato's Atlantis, at least the possibility that some such land mass had once existed, located, moreover, where he said it once flourished, beyond the Pillars of Hercules.

Renaissance scholars, familiar again with Greek learning, now re-examined Plato's description of this lost Atlantean world, and many of them soon convinced themselves that Columbus had discovered it where the Greek philosopher had said it was. Disregarding both the actual details given by Plato and disregarding even more historical and geographical considerations, the supporters of the American theory of Atlantis invented all sorts of corroboratory evidence to justify their beliefs; and this, of course, has been characteristic of the 2,000 year-old controversy. Petty little circumstantial clues like the discovery of a place named Aztlan in Mexico were eagerly pounced on as 'proof'; and on the basis of similar coincidences, ridiculous theories were promulgated by 18th-century scholars even of the calibre of Georges Buffon, the French naturalist, and later Alexander von Humboldt, the physician.

But these early speculations as to the whereabouts of the empire that vanished beneath the waves were based more upon their authors' imagination than upon any physical evidence, which is understandable considering the state of geographical and geological knowledge at the time. In fact, savants advocated their pet theory by means of odds and ends of erudition mostly picked up from the classical geographers – ideas such as the Mediterranean sea having been formed by the Atlantic

Ocean bursting in from the west via the Straits of Gibraltar and the Indian Ocean from the east via the Red Sea and the Gulf of Suez. In contrast, the Swedish scientist Olof Rudbeck, a man of immense learning and the discoverer of the lymphatic system, preferred to ransack the Icelandic sagas of the 13th century in search of clues – notably *Snorri's Edda* and *Saemund's Edda* – to 'prove' that Atlantis was situated in his homeland near Uppsala in Sweden.

The 19th-century approach to the problem of locating the now famous island was, on the face of it, altogether more 'scientific' as advances in geography, and particularly in geology, added enormously to our knowledge of the earth's conformation. In addition, a logical system of prehistory had been developed. The searchers after Atlantis were not slow to use the new knowledge to support new theories, so that the 19th and early 20th centuries were the golden age of the Atlantophiles or, as their detractors refer to them, the Atlantomaniacs.

Yet it was easy enough for the sceptics to discredit all attempts to find Atlantis on the grounds that pedants like Olof Rudbeck made a nonsense of Plato's report. The fact remained that many learned and well-balanced observers kept an open mind concerning the controversy, and one would hardly accuse William Ewart Gladstone of being a crank when he suggested that it would be an exercise useful to both scholarship and practical oceanography to equip an exploration ship to study the problem.

The problem, then, has been seriously studied and

continues to occupy a whole variety of experts – historians, archaeologists, geologists, oceanographers, vulcanologists, and classical scholars; and far from being dismissed as a 'noble lie' is beginning to be accepted as the shadowy outline of one of the most spectacular events in history. It is for this reason that the search for Atlantis constitutes such a fascinating chapter in the annals of discovery.

## 2: AMATEUR EXPLORERS OF ATLANTIS

THE basic facts about Atlantis as given by Plato are, of course, the 'clues' which detectives, amateur and professional, must follow in order to solve the mystery of the whereabouts of the lost kingdom.

(1) Atlantis was an island beyond the Pillars of Hercules and somewhere in the Atlantic Ocean.

(2) It was larger than Libya and Asia put together. (By Libya, Greek geographers in Plato's time meant the North African hinterland from the frontiers of Egypt to the Atlantic Ocean. By Asia they meant, in general, the Middle East. They had no clear idea of the true area of these territories.)

(3) Beyond Atlantis, a chain of islands led to an opposite continent which surrounded the true Ocean.

This appears to be a reference to the Americas, but Plato, of course, had no inkling of the existence of the New World. His cosmography was based on philosophical speculation so that an atlas of the world as it was conceived in the 4th century BC would look something like Figure 1.

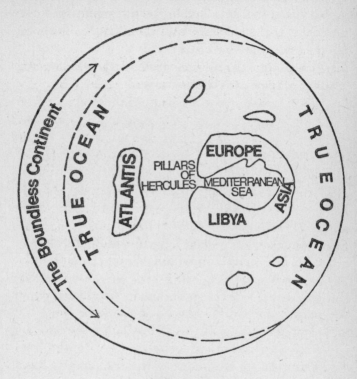

FIGURE 1

## THE WORLD ACCORDING TO PLATO

So much for the geographical location of Atlantis. Plato gives two other important geophysical facts which are significant for searchers after his island. He says:

(4) After the defeat of the invaders from Atlantis by the Athenians, there occurred violent earthquakes and floods, and in a single day and night of terror all the armies involved in the war were wiped out and the island itself disappeared in the depths of the sea.

(5) As a result of the subsidence of this large land mass, that area of the Atlantic where Atlantis once existed is shallow and marked by shoals. (In view of the Greek ignorance of the waters beyond the Straits of Gibraltar, Plato simply says 'the sea in those parts is impassable and impenetrable because there is a shoal of mud in the way'.)

If all the information Plato gives us were this specific, the question of reality or myth would be easier to answer. It has long been known that whole islands rise from and disappear under the sea as a result of volcanic eruption or submarine earthquakes. And the further back in geological time we go, the more we see that continents and seas have changed their conformation, Plato, in fact, actually goes back 9,000 years before Solon's time (the 6th century BC) to account for the cataclysm which destroyed Atlantis.

But it is at this point that we run into serious difficulties and that an impartial observer finds it impossible to accept the story as the literal truth. The plain fact is that Plato's description cannot conceivably square with the findings of modern science. Remembering, for instance, that the events he relates took place, according to his chronology, around 12,000 BC (i.e. from our own date) we are carried back in time to

the Stone Age. How was it possible, then, for the Atlanteans on the one hand and the Athenians on the
other to have such an advanced technological and
urban civilization which we do not find anywhere else
in the world until around 4,000 BC at the very earliest
when we see the first signs of an advanced society in
the Land of Sumer?

We have discussed earlier some of the characteristics
which Plato ascribes to Atlantis – the nature of the
island, the kind of people who inhabited it, their archi-
tecture, arts, religion, and so forth. What the philosopher gives us *in part* is the description of a utopia
which, like other utopias dreamt of by visionaries, is a
moral fable not concerned with physical time at all.
And we should note at this point that Plato's chronology, like his geography, need not be taken as accurate
or final at all. Any sort of statistics in ancient texts are
questionable even if only because they may have been
copied wrongly by scribes. Still, those Atlantophiles[3]
who have tried to explain away the difficulties or dis-
crepancies of Plato's story suggest that the 9,000 years
meant 9,000 months by Egyptian reckoning, which
gives us a much more acceptable figure of 750 years.
Add 750 to 550 BC, the approximate year of Solon's
visit to Egypt, and we are well within the period of
historical records – 1,300 BC. The student can, of course,
accept or reject such reckoning.

We have mentioned above the number of places where
Atlantis has been 'found', and it only now remains to
summarize some of the more unusual as well as more

feasible of the theories so that other students can take up the challenge if they so wish.

The theories fall into roughly three categories: the literary, the geological, and the historical, though the three approaches to the problems are not, of course, mutually exclusive.

Let us examine some of the more outstanding theories, beginning with those derived more or less from literary or mythological sources combined with a great deal of personal 'intuition'.

In 1912, Dr Paul Schliemann, the grandson of Heinrich Schliemann, the discoverer of Troy, announced in an American newspaper that he had discovered the secret of Atlantis, 'the source of all civilization'. He had been able to do so, he said, with the aid of documents hidden in a Phoenician vase. In view of his grandfather's extraordinary achievement – the revelation that Troy was an actual place and not a mythical city invented by Homer – the public was ready and eager to listen to his descendant.

Dr Schliemann elected to tell his fantastic story in the *New York American*, an odd medium for a scholar, but not as odd as the article itself entitled 'How I Discovered Atlantis'. In this article Schliemann stated that his grandfather left a number of secret papers sealed in envelopes on which was written 'only to be opened after my death'. One of these envelopes contained Heinrich Schliemann's 'Atlantis documents', but his grandson did not know which envelope, except that the world-famous archaeologist had scribbled a note on his death-bed indicating that the secret of Atlantis would be found in an 'owl-headed vase'. In addition, the dying man abjured that member of the family to whom the secret was entrusted to dedicate his life to completing the research whose findings to date would be found in the sealed envelope.

Grandson Paul was the lucky member of the family to inherit the documents pertaining to Atlantis as well as the owl-headed vase, so it was the privilege and duty to pledge himself to continue his grandfather's work.

How far then, had the discoverer of Troy progressed in his search for Atlantis? According to his grandson, to the point where he could prove the actual existence of that island on the basis of firm archaeological evidence; for among the notes Heinrich had made was a reference to a great bronze vase unearthed during the Trojan excavations and containing among other things artefacts inscribed in the Phoenician script with the words, *From King Cronos of Atlantis*.

And what about the contents of the owl-headed vase of Phoenician provenance? According to Paul, it contained a sort of medallion of a metal like silver with the inscription, again in Phoenician, *Issued in the Temple of Transparent Walls*. Significantly, he does not say what else he found inside this mysterious vase.

Armed with these valuable clues and mindful of his duty to his famous grandfather, Paul writes in *The New York American* that he set to work to examine the Atlantis problem which had puzzled men ever since Plato gave the details of the lost island to the world more than 2,000 years before, and that his investigations had finally led him to the solution. His methods and results, he implied, were consistent with the highest academic standards as would be expected of the grandson of Schliemann of Troy and a doctor of philosophy in his (Paul's) own right. Not only had the literature of the ancient western and eastern worlds been carefully investigated, but also that of the New World. In short, he now claimed that Greek, Phoenician, Chaldaean, and Mayan texts were shown to have had a common origin which could only be logically explained in terms of a prototype culture, namely, that of Atlantis lying midway between the Old and the New Worlds. Dr Schliemann states that he was particularly fortunate in coming across first, a Chaldaean manuscript which had been smuggled out of a Buddhist temple in Lhasa and secondly, the Troano Codex or Mayan text in the British Museum.[4] He had translated these two books and discovered that both of them described a cataclysm which overwhelmed a country called Mu. What, he asks, is the significance of two accounts of the same event, one from Central America, the other from Central Asia if it did not postulate the existence of a parent culture in the Atlantic? Dr Schliemann promised in the American newspaper to give the answer to this and all other questions concerning Atlantis in a forthcoming book. The book, however, never appeared. In fact, Paul Schliemann was openly denounced as an impostor by his German critics, one of whom, Wilhelm Dörpfeld, was a collaborator of the celebrated grandfather, and Paul and his owl-headed vase containing the silver medallion inscribed in Phoenician, the great bronze urn unearthed at Troy, the artefacts carrying references to King Cronos of Atlantis, and the Chaldaean manuscript from Lhasa, Tibet, all disappeared from the scene shortly after the publication of the sensational article in the *New York American*.

Perhaps the reasons are obvious. In the first place, Heinrich Schliemann was known to have only a slight interest in Atlantis and to have made no specific inquiries into the subject. Secondly, nobody other than Paul saw the vase, urn, and other artefacts which he claimed were left him by his grandfather. Thirdly, no one has yet succeeded in convincing the philologists that he can read the Mayan language.

But though Dr Schliemann had his detractors, he could at least be said to have stimulated interest in cultures other than those derived from the Mediterranean civilizations.

In fact, even before Paul Schliemann announced his discovery, a new school of ethnology had arisen, which looked westwards for the origins of civilization instead of eastwards across the Atlantic. The latest theories were partially based on Plato's assertion that the invading Atlanteans came from an island to the *west*, a land which was one of the stepping stones to the 'true continent' on the other side of the Ocean, whence it was argued that since the inhabitants of Atlantis sailed eastwards, conquering and colonizing the mainland of Europe, they could equally well have sailed westwards to the Americas on the same mission. If so, was there any evidence of an advanced civilization in the Americas, which was brought to those shores by a mid-Atlantic people? Or, alternatively, did civilization come to the Old World from the New via the Atlantis staging post?

Dr Augustus Le Plongeon, a Franco-American physician, was one of those who believed that it did. He published his findings in 1896, in a book entitled *Queen Moo and the Egyptian Sphinx*. 'The solution of that much mooted question among modern scientists,' he says in the preface to *Queen Moo*, 'namely, the existence, destruction, and submergence of a large island in the Atlantic Ocean, as related by Plato in his *Timaeus* and *Critias*, is found in the Mayan writings.'[5]

Four different authors, he claims, have left descriptions of the famous cataclysm, two surviving in manuscript form as codices known as Troana and Cortesianus; a third being engraved on stone in a temple at Chichen; and a fourth written thousands of miles from Central America in Athens itself, this one in the form of an epic poem in the Mayan language.

It was the third of these which Dr Le Plongeon claimed he was able to read 'because it is written with hieratic Maya characters that are likewise Egyptian. Anyone who can read hieratic Egyptian inscriptions will have no difficulty in translating said legend by the aid of a Maya dictionary.'[6]

The doctor's assertion that Mayan hieroglyphs are the same as Egyptian is not shared by the specialists in either language or, for that matter, can such a claim be accepted by any student who takes the trouble to

consult the Troano Codex itself. A pre-Columbian
Mayan manuscript, the Troano is one of four books
which survived the holocaust which Bishop Landa
describes in his *Relación* of 1565. 'We found in the
possession of the Mayas a large number of books written in these letters of theirs and, as they contained
nothing in which there was not some superstition and
devil's lies, we burnt them all, at which they felt wondrous sorrow and were grieved.'[7]

Two of these books, the Troana and the Cortesian,
are in Madrid; a third is in Dresden; and a fourth in
Paris. All four come not from Yucatan, as Dr Le Plongeon says, but from farther south in a region where the
bow and arrow were unknown and the principal weapons were lances, darts, axes, and shields. All four were
probably written some time in the 14th or 15th centuries of our era, but their contents are obviously much
older. It is now fairly well agreed that these books deal
with mythological matters as well as the Calendar
(always an important subject to early peoples), agriculture, locust plagues, hunting, weaving, music, and
head-shrinking. To examine the Troano Codex is a
fascinating experience since one can almost grasp the
sense of it in places through the beautiful drawings of
gods, kings, warriors, and animals. Alongside the drawings are what seem to be pictographs or ideographs,
having no resemblance at all to Egyptian hieroglyphs,
as Dr Le Plongeon claims. One wonders if he had ever
seen any of the four Mayan manuscripts or, for that
matter, what was his competence to translate the sacred
writing of the ancient Egyptians.

So all we can say of the Mayan books is that they are probably manuscripts of magic written for and by the priests who used ideograms as mnemonic devices in the manner of all early writing, including that of Easter Island. Many of the signs are frequently repeated which should be a clue to cryptographers – for instance:

What appear to be numbers are found on every page, written as circles and horizontal bars:

Dr Le Plongeon's attempts at reading the Mayan manuscripts and the inscriptions on the extant monuments led him to the discovery or, as some claimed, the invention, of the 'Land of Mu', which he identifies with Plato's Atlantis, adding 'Let us hope that no one will be so bold as to accuse Plato of having been in collusion with the author of the Troano MS.[8] The doctor evidently had in mind the resemblance between some of the Greek and some of the Mayan descriptions of the cataclysm. The latter, as found in the Troano Codex, he translates as:

The country of the hills of mud, the Land of Mu, was sacrificed. Being twice upheaved, it suddenly disappeared during the night, the oasis being continually shaken by volcanic forces. Being confined, these caused the land to

sink and rise several times and in various places. At last
the surface gave way, and the ten countries were torn
asunder and scattered in fragments; unable to withstand
the force of the seismic convulsions, they sank with their
sixty-four millions of inhabitants, 8,060 years before the
writing of this book.[9]

According to Dr Le Plongeon, then, the real name
of Atlantis was Mu, which was merely another colony
of the Mayans, who first brought civilization to Europe,
Africa, and Asia – in fact, to the entire world. Mayan
navigators visited the shores of every continent, their
warriors conquered lands as distant as Japan, and Mu
was simply a stage-post, as it were, in the Atlantic
route to the Mediterranean – a detail which agrees
with Plato's description of Atlantis as the jumping-off
point for the great invasion of 9,500 BC. Apart from
this area of agreement, however, Dr Plongeon and
Plato tell widely different stories of the lost island,
perhaps because the former was an advocate of the
superiority of American culture, the latter of European.

In this respect, the theories of Dr Le Plongeon and
his American followers counter-balance the speculations of European scholars who, like Dr Olof Rudbeck,[10] placed Atlantis somewhere in Sweden, or of
Jurgen Spanuth[11] who traced it to the island of Heligoland, or of Karl Georg Zschaetzsch[12] who claimed it
was the homeland of the pure Aryan race, a blond,
blue-eyed people who had created a high moral civilization eventually vitiated by intermarriage with non-
Aryan, or lesser breeds. Thus, according to Zschaetzsch,

it was a non-Aryan woman who degraded man by first brewing fermented drinks, as Eve suborned him with her apple.

So just as many Atlantean theorists attracted a following by associating Plato's utopian island with a particular homeland or a racial attitude, so Dr Le Plongeon's Mayan hypothesis had considerable influence in the late 19th-century United States, where national pride seems to have been flattered by the proofs, derived from the New York physician's translations of the Mayan pictograms, that America was the source of world civilization. His work also focused attention on the Polynesian peoples whose culture was conceivably linked up through the Mayans to the culture of the western world, and from this hypothesis arose still another Atlantean-type lost world called Lemuria, discussed in the next chapter.

The theories put forward by Dr Le Plongeon were either totally ignored or received in polite silence by serious students of the Atlantis myth, which is understandable in view of the rather quarrelsome tone the doctor assumes in his book and, even more, his predilection for statements like 'Jesus spoke Maya' and 'the Chaldaeans, as we have shown, were in their origin a Maya colony who used the metre as their standard of linear measures'.[13] All these assertions are, of course, arrant nonsense just as the doctor's personal attacks on contemporary ethnologists today make tiresome reading.

However, his book, *Queen Moo and the Egyptian*

*Sphinx*, was, in its own eccentric fashion, a collateral work with the much more impressive opus of Ignatius Donnelly, the brilliant, self-educated American lawyer and politician whose *Atlantis: the Antediluvian World*, first published in 1882, is a classic of Atlantean literature. In fact, Donnelly and his successor, Lewis Spence, restored dignity as well as scholarship to the field of Atlantean studies which so easily became a playground for impostors.

Some idea of the importance of Donnelly's book, as well as the popular interest in the subject, can be gathered from the world-wide acclaim it received and, even more, from the fact that it has never been superseded as a statement of the common cultural origin of early peoples on both sides of the Atlantic. To prove his thesis, Donnelly examined in a rational and scientific spirit the religious beliefs and actual artefacts of the ancient civilizations of Egypt on the one hand and Central America on the other, and concluded from his studies that there were enough similarities between the two to make the existence of a common fructifying culture essential. That common denominator was, he argued, Atlantis, the motherland of colonies on both sides of the ocean.

The essence of Donnelly's theory is that a lost continent now sunk below the waves exactly where Plato located it geographically, sent out colonists to both northern and southern Europe, north and central America, the west coast of Africa, and the eastern Mediterranean and so exported its customs and skills to all those countries. (One can compare the wide distribution of the British way of life throughout the Empire during the Victorian period, so that archaeologists, turning up a cricket stump in Fiji in 5,000 years' time, might well be puzzled as to how and why it got there.)

He also attempted 'to demonstrate several distinct and novel propositions' one of which was that

Atlantis was the true Mediterranean world; the Garden of Eden, the Garden of the Hesperides – where the Atlantides lived on the River Ocean in the west; the Elysian fields – situated by Homer to the west of the Earth, the Gardens of Alcinous, grandson of Poseidon and son of Nausithous, King of the Phaeacians of the Island of Scheria; the Mesomphalis – or Navel of the Earth, a name given to the Temple of Delphi, which was situated in the crater of an extinct volcano; the Mount Olympus of the Greeks; the Asgard of the Eddas; the focus of the tradition of the ancient nations; representing a universal memory of a great land where early mankind dwelt for ages in peace and happiness.[14]

The author set about demonstrating this and his other propositions in twenty-four chapters whose titles show the sobriety and scholarship of his approach to the problem. Chapter Five, for instance, deals with 'The Testimony of the Sea'; Chapter Six, 'The Testimony of the Flora and Fauna'; other chapters with such subjects as the Deluge Legends, a comparison of the civilizations of the Old and the New Worlds, mummification, the Bronze and Iron Ages, and the origin of our alphabet.

For us, a hundred years later, Ignatius Donnelly's

treatise is a typical example of what his latest editor calls 'one of the last outbursts of learning before the world was swamped with mediocrity'.[15] In other words, it is packed with many obscure and fascinating facts which were the results of the author's wide reading in a great and scholarly library such as the Library of Congress. But the most important contribution that Donnelly made to Atlantology was to make the subject a 'respectable' discipline, related to such legitimate studies as geology, mythology, philology, and so forth. In other words, this American scholar rescued Plato's story from the limbo of pseudo-science to which it had been relegated from the 4th century BC, making the very name of Atlantis almost anathema to serious-minded scholars like Benjamin Jowett. Perhaps if it had not been for Donnelly's book, the whole subject would, by this time, have been relegated to the scientific ragbag along with astrology and alchemy. But his study was immediately recognized by all educated people as a serious presentation and examination of the evidence on the basis of which readers were invited to draw their own conclusions. Many readers, including Gladstone, as we have already mentioned, were convinced that the American had proved the truth of Plato's story. Atlantis had, after all, existed; it only remained to find the ultimate proof somewhere beneath the Atlantic waves.

Ignatius Donnelly, then, was the Father of Scientific Atlantology and all *rational* research had followed the paths which he first signposted. His disciples appeared all over the world after his immensely popular book had been translated into the principal European languages. Schools of Atlantologists and Societies of Atlanteans were formed, some of them serious, some of them mock-serious. The French, for instance, founded an Atlantean society which split into two groups, one emphasizing the intellectual aspects of their hobby, the other the social, so that there was a choice of attending a lecture with the first group or going on a picnic with the second.

In England, Donnelly's book was taken much more soberly. It inspired scholars of the rank and prestige of Lewis Spence, the Scottish mythologist (1874–1955) and an authority on ancient Mexico, to delve still more deeply into the folklore of primitive peoples. And if such researchers discovered nothing else, they at least demonstrated the universality of such legends as the Deluge and the concept of the Garden of Eden.

Lewis Spence is probably the last of that school of Atlantologists who base their theories on a literal acceptance of the location and time specified by Plato – the last because there is really nothing much more to say after the thorough investigations both he and Donnelly made into the folklore, religions, languages, and artefacts of the Old and New worlds. Their argument is very specific and is supported by a great deal of evidence which they invite the reader to examine for himself : namely, that there was once a land-bridge between Europe and America which was largely destroyed by various cataclysms, leaving only remnants in the form of island chains, the Azores, Madeira Islands, the Canaries, Cape Verde Islands, and the West Indies.

These islands, in other words, are the tips of mountain ranges whose sides have been submerged leaving only the highest peaks above water. Elsewhere in the ocean, running from north to south, lies the mid-Atlantic Ridge where the depth of water is only 50–60 fathoms as against 600 fathoms in Nares Deep to the west.

It was this land-bridge, they assert, which accounts for the affinities in culture between Egypt and Central America, a plausible theory which still inspires amateur oceanographers to look for submarine vestiges of the lost land mass.

The emphasis now shifted to the geological evidence. What could the experts, for instance, prove about the submarine conformation of the Atlantic? Some of the more cynical observers of the controversy replied that geologists can prove pretty much what they want concerning prehistoric events, including a land-bridge which joined Morocco to Central America. Others, again, were convinced that some time during the Miocene epoch, twenty-seven million years ago, volcanic eruptions tore apart an Atlantic land mass, leaving only those island chains which still exist today. And as if to complicate the issue still further, still other theorists came forward with the 'evidence' for *two* lost continents, one in the eastern Atlantic called Atlantis, the other in the western Atlantic called Antillia. All that remains of the former land mass are the islands off the coast of Africa; and of the latter, the archipelago known as the Lesser and Greater Antilles.

The difficulties of these geological theories is, of

course, that we have now been carried back in time to an epoch before man made his appearance on the scene, let alone was the highly civilized creature whom Plato describes. And it was this incontrovertible fact which forced Lewis Spence and his followers to shift their ground and to narrow down their search for Atlantis to the post-glacial stage: that is, to around 30,000 BC, when a race of men inhabited the caves of southern France and north-western Spain where they left a record of their activities in their fabulous drawings at sites like Lascaux and Altamira. According to Spence, these men, if they themselves did not originate in Atlantis, nonetheless received their artistic and technical skills from that centre of civilization. Then, 10,000 years ago, there was still another influx of Atlanteans into western Europe – this time a race ethnologists refer to as Azilians, who were always buried with their faces towards the west. Was this significant custom due to the fact that their original homeland lay in the direction of the setting sun somewhere out in the Atlantic? And, if so, were they the survivors of that disaster which overwhelmed Atlantis exactly in the manner and at the time Plato describes?

Lewis Spence's arguments kept geologists, ethnologists, and pre-historians quite busy presenting new or demolishing old evidence; but, at the same time there were also other challenging geological, geophysical, and even astronomical theories which occupied the attentions of Atlantologists. The most notable of these propositions was the cosmological theory of Hans Hoerbiger of Vienna. Hoerbiger, who according to some commentators was a genius, according to others an impostor, produced in 1913 the sensational theory that the moon was not a satellite of the earth but a separate planet which moved around the sun in its own rather erratic orbit. About 15,000 years ago the moon, which for a long time had been coming closer to the earth, was finally captured by our planet's gravitational pull and from that time on ceased to be an independent planet and became a satellite of earth.

But this remarkable cosmic event was not accomplished without the most violent changes in the shape and configuration of our globe. The earth was squeezed, as it were, into its present elliptic shape; its crust was split open; volcanoes erupted; and seismic tremors convulsed the earth's surface along the lines of fracture. Even more stupendous than these violent changes was the behaviour of the oceans and seas now pulled by tremendous forces from the polar latitudes towards the equator, there to be piled up like a huge wave before receding again as the captured moon took up its new orbit, when its gravitational pull on the waters of the earth began to regulate the tides as we know them today.

If Hans Hoerbiger is right then, and the moon far from being a satellite torn out of the body of the earth is a 'captured' planet, the folklore of floods and great disasters preserved in myths all over the world are an echo of that time when most of our world, with everything in it, was destroyed by fire and water; when the entire 'Atlantic' ocean was inundated by a flood tide thousands of feet deep. It was this catastrophe which is recorded in the Hebrew myth of Noah and his ark, the Greek fable of Deucalion and his ark, and the Egyptian story of Atlantis as told to Plato. True, no reputable astronomer today accepts Hoerbiger's theory as anything but the dream – or some would say nightmare – of a visionary. But his ideas continue to excite that school of Atlantologists who insist that Atlantis lies somewhere beneath the waves of the western ocean.

One of the myths, incidentally, which is said to support the Hoerbiger theory is the Revelation of St John the Divine. In the 17th and 18th chapters of that apocalyptic book the downfall of Babylon is interpreted by the supporters of the so-called glacial cosmogony as referring to the destruction of Atlantis, even though Biblical exegetes maintain that Revelation was written by some unidentified early Christian pastor who was much more concerned with prophesying the future of the Church than with relating the pagan past. Not so, says H. S. Bellamy, the leader of the occult school of Atlantologists; St John the Divine was a scholar learned in astrosophy, symbolology, numerology, and many other hermetic sciences and he obtained his Revelations from ancient books which contained reports of great cosmic convulsions.

Mr Bellamy also sees in the old Icelandic saga *Edda* further confirmation of the Hoerbiger lunar thesis, particularly in the most ancient of these poems, the Völuspa, or Prophecy of the Sibyl. In this chant we hear the words of an inspired prophetess 'seated on her throne, addressing Odin while the gods listen to her words'.

Here again, as in the case of the *Book of Revelations*, opinion depends very much on a subjective interpretation of the text. Where orthodox scholars see a primitive dithyrambic type of folk literature whose meaning escapes or confuses us – all those lamps, candlesticks, brass wind instruments, eyes and horns of animals never seen in any zoo but appearing in every other paragraph of the *Revelations*; and where in the Edda the giants, dwarfs, thralls, churls, jarls and so forth seem to belong to another world entirely – the mystics find it all clear provided the normal processes of logical thinking are dispensed with.

And this reliance on 'revelation' is characteristic of the school of Atlantology which bases its theories almost entirely on the evidence of myths. In brief, the occultists insist that Plato's report is essentially true in all its details and that we must therefore look for Atlantis where he said it was – in the Atlantic Ocean. In contrast, many eminent scholars of a more scientific turn of mind disregard Plato's geography and look for sites they consider more feasible on archaeological grounds. In this connection, various theories, some 'scientific' and some merely fanciful, were put forward by French and German African explorers, particularly in the last quarter of the 19th century when the Sahara was just beginning to be opened up by the French camel corps. Some of the ideas advocated by these African travellers owe more to a romantic than a factual view of history and are epitomized by the celebrated novel by Pierre Benoît, *Atlantide*, which led to the 'discovery' of the city of Antinea, the queen of Atlantis, by Count Byron

Khun de Prorok at a place called Abelessa in southern Algeria. The present writer has visited this so-called city, which is of considerable interest to historians of the Sahara since it is a very early fort dating back perhaps to the period of the Roman occupation of North Africa. It was undoubtedly a stronghold of the Tuareg and contained the tomb of a rich and important woman, buried with her jewels and personal possessions. She may even have been Tin Hinan, the legendary queen of the Tuareg, but she was certainly not the queen of the island kingdom which Plato describes.[16]

Other African locations suggested as the site of Atlantis are Tunisia, favoured by the French geologist Paul Borchardt and the German historian Albert Hermann; the Central Sahara explored by Henri Lhote; the Yoruba country of Nigeria, advocated by Leo Frobenius, the German anthropologist; Morocco, preferred by the French archaeologist, Felix Berlious; and at the other extreme of the Afro-Asian continent the orientalist Josef Karst placed Atlantis somewhere in the Persian Gulf from whence, he argues, came those prehistoric migrations of an Indo-Atlantic race of dolmen builders.[17]

There were, too, a number of scholars who argued for European locations. The most convincing on the basis of the historical evidence was Tartessos, the ancient city called Tarshish in the Bible. Tartessos is thought to have been situated at the mouth of the river Guadalquivir in south-western Spain, north of Cadiz. At the beginning of the Bronze Age, it was the clearing-house of the Phoenician fleets carrying British, French, and Spanish tin and copper to the factories in the Eastern Mediterranean. Yet even though the existence of Tartessos is attested by Greek and Roman geographers as well as by the Old Testament writers, the site of the city has never been found despite intensive excavations. Nonetheless the German historians Adolf Schulten and Richard Rennig were convinced that Tartessos was the capital of Atlantis which Plato described as rich in metals and the centre of civilization beyond the Pillars of Hercules. This theory was further developed by Mrs E. M. Wishaw, an amateur archaeologist, who had been searching for material evidence of Tartessos for a quarter of a century and eventually claimed to have found it in the Rio Tinto copper mines which, she said, were exploited by neolithic men. From her researches she deduced that the Tartessian kingdom was not itself Atlantis, but a colony planted on the mainland by the Atlanteans from 12,000–14,000 years ago.[18]

The French botanist Dr Ferdinand Gidon produces quite different arguments for another European site: he chooses the English Channel between Ireland and Brittany as the location of an Atlantis submerged by a great inundation during the Bronze Age. His evidence, based on the occurrence of plant species and climatic changes during the pre-historic period in northern Europe, was acquired as a result of asking whether the Atlantis myth could not have originated from the reports received in southern Europe of submergences which had taken place along the northern coasts, particularly off the coasts of Brittany and Ireland. He concluded that Atlantis and the flourishing civilization that Plato ascribed to it referred to a Bronze Age culture in North Europe.

And so we find the site of Atlantis placed farther and farther to the north, particularly by those researchers who consciously or subconsciously desired to identify this archetypal civilization with their own nation. We have already referred to the German Karl Georg Zschaetzsch who identified the Atlanteans with the primal blue-eyed, blond and clean-living Aryans, anticipating by some years the Nazi theory of the German superman.[19] And in recent years another German, Jürgen Spanuth, has traced the capital of Atlantis to a submarine city called Basileia off the island of Heligoland. Mr Spanuth claims to have brought up paving stones from the submerged city which help to prove his theory that the victorious North people swept across Europe as far as Egypt because they were forced to leave their island homes in an age of terrible catastrophes.[20]

Reviewing these various theories as to the location of Atlantis, the observer is struck by the fact that the protagonists of even the most exotic suggestions have often been scholars or specialists. In other words, Atlantology despite the obvious fact that it has attracted a great many eccentrics has nonetheless attracted the attention of many of the world's best minds, as, of course, it attracted the interest of Plato himself.

And yet one cannot escape the feeling aroused by

many of the hypotheses, well-argued though they may be, that logic, reason, and the facts themselves have frequently been adapted to fit what seems to have begun as a 'hunch'. We see this process in operation in the occult theories of Atlantis in which something called 'astral clairvoyance' is employed to investigate the events of our planet in prehistoric epochs. Astral clairvoyance enabled its practitioners to describe a creature called a Lemurian Man as follows:

His stature was gigantic, somewhere between twelve and fifteen feet. . . . He had a long lower jaw, a strangely flattened face, eyes small but piercing and set curiously far apart, so that he could see sideways as well as in front, while the eye at the back of his head – on which part of the head no hair of course grew – enabled him to see in that direction also. . . . In his right hand was twisted the end of a long rope made of some sort of creeping plant, by which he held a huge and hideous reptile, somewhat resembling the plesiosaurus. The Lemurians actually domesticated these creatures and trained them to employ their strength in hunting other animals.[21]

We shall be discussing the lost continent of Lemuria and the people who inhabited it in the next chapter. We refer to it now as an example of the psychic or occult approach to the story of Atlantis in contradistinction to a purely scientific inquiry. Many serious Atlantologists censure the former attitude as fantastic or even frivolous, the kind of amateurish dabbling which brings the subject into disrepute. What, of course, is certain is that no amount of investigation can ever prove – or disprove – the existence of such lost lands as Lemuria or can ever trace the footprints of those men of Mu who stood around fifteen feet high and had an eye in the back of their head. These humanoids belong with the Africans described by Pliny as having their heads in the middle of their chests.

On the other hand, *factual* evidence for the existence of Plato's Atlantis continues to be presented almost every year, to be accepted by some as conclusive, rejected by others as unconvincing. The latest and most scientifically orthodox theory which may finally solve the mystery once and for all is that of the professional archaeologists, supported by the historians, geologists, and vulcanologists – an imposing body of savants whose training and academic standing do not encourage them to indulge in fantasy or idle speculation.

These specialists believe that they have finally identified Atlantis. The evidence and the methods by which they follow the available clues form the subject of another chapter. But first, we shall examine some other theories which, while they begin with the nucleus of the Atlantis story as told by Plato, take us to some new and still more curious lost worlds.

## 3: WAS IT LEMURIA? OR WAS IT MU?

THE Atlantis myth, as we have now seen, has motivated many famous scholars to use every resource of science in their search for the historical truth. Simultaneously, it has inspired others who believe that truth is more likely to be revealed by spiritual than by physical means. This group includes the theosophists, anthroposophists, yogis, and mystics in general.

While accepting Plato's *Timaeus* and *Critias* as valuable, the occultists claim access to still older documents, documents which they assert have turned up all over the world, the favourite locations being India, Tibet, and Central America. The most notable of these mysterious sources is the *Akashic Records* which Rudolf Steiner, the Austrian founder of the Anthroposophical Society, states have several chapters referring to Atlantis; and, much more significant, these 'records' refer to a lost world even older than Atlantis: namely, the Land of Lemuria, an entire continent now sunk beneath the waters of the Pacific Ocean. The Lemurians, in fact, were the ancestors of the Atlanteans from whom modern man is descended, for according to the followers of Rudolf Steiner, there are, or will be before human evolution is complete, seven root-races of men: the first two are still unknown; the third was the Lemurians; the fourth, the Atlanteans; the fifth, the Aryans; and there are two more to come.

Where, then, is Lemuria? What is it? And how much about it do we know? The name was first suggested in 1855 by the English zoologist Philip Lutley Sclater who postulated an area in the Pacific as the aboriginal home of the *lemurs* – a region to which, he suggested, they have an atavistic urge to return. Sclater's theory appears to have been suggested by the contemporary scientific belief that the *lemmings* of Norway in their quadrennial suicide migration were attempting to return to their ancestral home on Atlantis. And no sooner had Sclater proposed an aboriginal habitat for the lemurs than geologists came forward prepared to support his contention, whence Lemuria was adopted as the name for an Atlantis of the Pacific. The logic here is interesting to a student of ideas. We start with the proposition that there might have been a land mass somewhere in the Pacific which would account for the world-wide distribution of the lemur; this suggestion is accepted as possible, even if unproven, by some geologists; the Theosophists, Anthroposophists, and other occultists thereupon name this undiscovered country Lemuria after the lemurs who may or may not have originated there; and mythologists favourable to the concept thereupon produce evidence of a lost land in the legends of the Pacific islanders; and within a very short time Lemuria is actually being drawn on the maps and discussed in books and articles.[22]

As a result, there were soon a number of specialists on Lemuria as there were on the equally mysterious Land of Mu; and in both cases, the historians of these lost continents relied heavily on inspiration, intuition, and various arcane documents. Madame Helena Blavatsky, the Russo-American founder of the Theosophical Society, for instance, now added the weight of her prestige to the controversy by accepting as proven what had hitherto been the mere speculation of a zoologist. Madame Blavatsky went one step farther: she invented a race of people as well as a geographical location for the lost world. Claiming that her information came from the ancient Indian wisdom-writings, the leader of the Theosophists stated that Lemuria occupied practically the entire southern hemisphere 'from the foot of the Himalayas to within a few degrees of the Antarctic Circle'. It was populated by a half-human race who mated with animals, though they themselves were bi-sexual and had an astral body only, together with a third eye in the back of their head which conferred on them psychic vision. These Lemurians and their continent were swept away before the Third Eocene Age, though their descendants survive as Australian aborigines, Papuans, and Hottentots.[23]

Concurrently, the Austrian Rudolf Steiner, who was associated for a time with Mme Blavatsky's Theosophical movement until he broke away to form his own Anthroposophical Society, took many of his notions regarding Lemuria, its location, inhabitants, and culture from *The Secret Doctrine* of Mme Blavatsky, though he added some new and exciting details which he had acquired by consulting what he called the *Akashic Records*.[24] From these documents he learnt that the Lemurians had no spoken language, but were able to communicate with each other by thought-transference. Similarly, they were able to do whatever was necessary by will-power alone, so that whereas they were still physically in an embryonic stage of evolution and had no proper brain, they were able to move mountains if they wished, as well as to build enormous 'erections' devoted to the service of 'Divine Wisdom and Divine Art'. Consequently, though they were at the cultural level of cavemen (for they lived in caves and the holes in the ground made by their excavations), they were able to defy the forces of nature in addition to enjoying intercourse with the gods.

The next leading authority on Lemuria was the British Theosophist, W. Scott-Elliott, who produced a set of maps in 1906 which showed the outlines of Atlantis and Lemuria at six critical stages of their history: (1) about 1,000,000 years ago; (2) after the first catastrophe of 800,000 BC; (3) after the second catastrophe of 200,000 BC; (4) after the catastrophe of 80,000 BC; (5) Lemuria at its greatest extent (no date given); and (6) Lemuria 'at a later period'.

Scott-Elliott does not tell us where he obtained the data to compile these atlases except to say that the maps of Atlantis were produced by 'mighty Adepts in the days of Atlantis' and those of Lemuria 'by some of the divine instructors in the days when Lemuria still existed'. He does state, however, that 'it has been the great privilege of the writer to be allowed copies – more or less complete – of four of these atlases. All four represent Atlantis.'[25] We must take his word for it since the 'globe, a good bas-relief in terra-cotta, and a well-preserved map on parchment, or skin of some sort' from which he copied his maps are not available to non-members of the Theosophical Society.

As for the Lemurians, Scott-Elliott agrees with Rudolf Steiner that they were the third of the seven root-races. He had, however, some additional information concerning the preceding races. The first root-race was not human, but was formed of 'astral matter'. The second approximated more to the human, though their bodies were 'composed of ether'. But the third root-race, of which the Lemurians were the original specimens, had developed into huge ape-like creatures who lived on Mars, the Earth, and Mercury. This man-animal had certain physical characteristics which have since been lost in the process of evolution: he had a third eye in the back of his head, for instance, and because of the shape of his feet with their elongated heels could walk backwards just as easily as forwards. In addition, he enjoyed a double sex-life, since he was hermaphroditic like the earth-worm or garden snail. At what period this bi-sexual Lemurian became a he- or she-Atlantean, which is the fourth root-race, is not yet known since 'the mystery of the How of the generation of the distinct sexes must be very obscure, as it [meaning presumably the answer to this problem] is the business of an embryologist'.[26]

A very important aspect of Scott-Elliott's history of Lemuria is his discovery that the Lemurians planted a colony in the Ashanti country of Western Nigeria. This colony, which was so isolated that it never mixed with lower types (i.e. brute beasts), evolved into a separate species of the fourth root-race with the help of an Adept who came from the planet Venus to instruct these Nigerian Atlanteans in the arts and sciences of civilization. It was these advanced Lemurians who were to bring Atlantis to its great heights during the Golden Age, about 80,000 years ago. It will surprise many students of history to learn that the Atlanteans of this period were using jet-propelled aeroplanes and, indeed, the 'jump-jet' plane which is still in its devel-

opmental stage in our own times. Scott-Elliott writing
in 1896 describes the propulsion of the Atlantean air-
boats as follows:

A strong heavy metal chest which lay in the centre of the
boat was the generator. Thence the force flowed through
two large flexible tubes to either end of the vessel, as well
as through eight subsidiary tubes fixed fore and aft to the
bulwarks. They had double opening as pointed vertically
both up and down. When the journey was about to begin,
the valves of the eight bulwark tubes which were pointed
downwards were opened – all the other valves were closed.
The current rushing through these impinged on the earth
with such force as to drive the boat upwards while the
air itself continued to supply the necessary fulcrum. When
a sufficient elevation was reached, the flexible tube at that
end of the vessel which pointed away from the desired
destination was brought into action, while by the partial
closing of the valves the current rushing through the eight
vertical tubes was reduced to the small amount required
to maintain the elevation reached.[27]

One can see from this extract how original were the
notions propounded by the Theosophists, including as
they did some of the most prophetic as well as sensational aspects of science-fiction; and it is not surprising
that people, particularly in America, began to see the
Lemurians themselves, as in due course they were to
see the visitors who arrived from outer space in flying
saucers. On 22 May 1932, for instance, the *Los Angeles
Times Star* published an article in its Sunday supple-
ment describing a colony of Lemurians who were living
on the slopes of Mount Shasta in Northern California.

The writer of this article states that he was told by the conductor of the *Shasta Limited*, the train on which he was travelling to Portland, Oregon, that the light he had seen on the mountain from the observation car was 'Lemurians holding ceremonials'; so he decided to 'equip himself for an expedition' into the wilderness of Mount Shasta to find these mysterious people whom he imagined had disappeared ages ago along with the Atlanteans. When the preparations for his expedition were complete, the explorer drove his car to the town of Weed where he discovered the existence of a 'mystic village'. He also found other investigators on the spot, all of whom assured him that Mount Shasta lit up morning, noon, and night as the Lemurians held their ceremonials. Moreover, no one had as yet managed to penetrate the 'sacred precincts' which were as forbidden to strangers as the holy city of Lhasa in Tibet – and if anyone had actually reached the mystic village, he had never returned to tell the tale. However, 'the eminent scientist Professor Edgar Lucin Larkin, with determined sagacity, penetrated the Shasta wilderness as far as he could – or dared – and then, cleverly, continued his investigations from a promontory with a powerful long-distance telescope.'

What the professor saw was a great temple in the heart of the mystic village, a marvellous work of carved marble and onyx, rivalling in beauty and architectural splendour the magnificence of the temples of Yucatan. The Lemurians themselves were a peaceful community, evidently content to live as their forebears had lived before Lemuria was swallowed up by the sea

The last descendants of the first inhabitants of the earth, they no longer had an eye in the back of their heads nor were they able to walk backwards as easily as forwards, because the people of Weed had occasionally met Lemurians in the village store and described them as 'tall, barefoot, noble-looking men, with close-cropped hair, dressed in spotless white robes'. They were most popular with the storekeepers, for they paid for the enormous quantities of sulphur, salt, and lard which they purchased with large gold nuggets worth much more than the merchandise. In addition to possessing a magnificent temple of marble and onyx and a mine from which they dug the gold nuggets, the Lemurians, according to the writer of the *Times Star* article, had 'the secret power of the Tibetan masters': that is, they were able to blend themselves with their surroundings and vanish at will. They also had scientific knowledge far in advance of ours, though after several hundreds of thousands of years in America (which they called 'Gustama'), they still had not forgotten their original homeland of Lemuria in whose honour they lit up Mount Shasta in their midnight ceremony.

As far as is known, this description in an American newspaper is the only eye-witness account we have of the Lemurians and to some extent even that is second-hand since the writer of the article obtained much of his information from the citizens of Weed which he made his headquarters for his expedition into what he called the wilderness of California. Unfortunately, no trace of the eminent scientist Professor Edgar L. Larkin who studied the Lemurians through his 'long-distance' telescope can be found in the reference books, and he himself apparently did not publish a report of his findings. Nor shall we apparently ever hear from the four or five other explorers who actually penetrated 'the invisible protective boundary' of the Lemurian colony, since either these pioneers never returned to tell the tale or they were too terrified to recount to the world what they saw for fear of reprisals by the last descendants of a vanished race.

Some of the occultists whose beliefs, as we have seen, were based on personal inspiration rather than on factual evidence still preferred as the original home-land of the Atlanteans the lost Central American continent discovered by Dr Augustus La Plongeon, whose book *Queen Moo and the Egyptian Sphinx* we have discussed above. This continent, christened by Dr Le Plongeon the 'Land of Mu', was now to become the monopoly of the American Colonel James Churchward who published a series of books on the subject, beginning with *The Lost Continent of Mu, the Motherland of Man,* first published in 1926. This volume was followed every few years by the later fruits of the Colonel's researches – the *Children of Mu, Cosmic Faces of Mu,* and *Sacred Symbols of Mu.*

Colonel Churchward tells us that he obtained the story of Mu from the 'Naacal Tablets', which he found secreted in the archives of an Indian monastery whose name and location he does not give us. The tablets, moreover, were written 'in the original tongue of mankind', a language, not surprisingly, understood by only two high priests in India. However, an old priest gave the American a kind of crash course in this aboriginal language, which enabled him to translate the long-hidden clay tablets of the Naacals. He discovered that the writings described in detail the creation of the earth, of man, and of the place where he first appeared – namely, Mu.

Continuing his researches in other monasteries (none of them specified or located), the Colonel learnt that Mu had extended across most of the Pacific until it 'vanished in a vortex of fire and water 12,000 years ago'. He found confirmation of the events recounted in the Naacal Tablets in Hindu epics, ancient Mayan books, the 'Lhasa Record', the cliff writings of the western states of North America, and the monuments scattered all over the Pacific Islands. It is apparent that Mu corresponds in many respects with Lemuria, but the Colonel's description being derived from so many sources not available to other investigators, is much more vivid than anything Mme Blavatsky, Rudolf Steiner, or even W. Scott-Elliott give us. He is able, for instance, to translate an Easter Island tablet to paint this picture of a spring day in Mu before the continent was blown up by an explosion in the great Central Gas Belt: 'Over the cool rivers, gaudy-winged butterflies hovered in the shade of the trees, rising and falling in fairy-like movements, as if better to view their painted beauty in nature's mirror. Darting hither and thither from flower to flower, hummingbirds made their short flights, glistening like living jewels in the rays of the sun.'[28]

One does rather get the impression from this extract that the Easter Island scribes had been strongly influenced by Victorian lady-novelists, though this, of course, was impossible.

When it comes to reporting plain facts, the tablets consulted by the American are more prosaic: we are told by the 'Lhasa Record and others', for instance, that the population of Mu was sixty-four million; the king's title was Ra Mu; the dominant race was white – 'an exceedingly handsome people'; there were seven main cities and so forth. The eventual destruction of Mu, according to the Colonel's reading of the 'Troana Manuscript in the British Museum', happened during one night – 'down, down, down, she went, into the mouth of hell.'[29] As the land rose and fell, quivered and shook, Colonel Churchward writes, the subterranean fires burst forth in clouds of roaring flames *three miles in diameter*. A thick black pall of smoke overshadowed the land; cities and all things living were destroyed; and, in the words of the *Codex Cortesianus* and the *Troano Manuscript*, 'agonized cries of "Mu save us!" filled the air'. All these vivid descriptions and details of the destruction of Mu by fire and fifty million square miles of water, were, incidentally, recorded by Colonel Churchward in 1926, some twenty years before the first atomic explosion which is the nearest thing we have seen, so far, to the going 'down, down, down into the mouth of hell'.

Not surprisingly, the only survivors of this cataclysm were a few wretched beings who crouched on islands of rock through the Pacific. Many of them were hopelessly insane, driven mad by sheer horror; others prayed for death to relieve them; others took to such savage practices as cannibalism.

Those who wish to examine further the theories of the American colonel will find that his standard book, *The Lost Continent of Mu*, has been recently re-issued in both America and England though it is not clear whether the readers of this book are enthusiastic for Mu or for science-fiction. This will no doubt largely depend on the extent to which one accepts Colonel Churchward's translations of the Naacal tablets and the other sacred writings of Mu. As no one else has been given access to these documents, it is difficult to assess their authenticity, as it is difficult to trace Dr Le Plongeon's Mayan texts and Rudolf Steiner's *Akashic Records*. And an additional complication for those seeking to choose between the Atlantic and Pacific Oceans as the location of the lost continents is the rivalry among the different schools of occultism. Colonel Churchward, for instance, dismisses as invalid Schliemann's contention that Mu and Atlantis were identical. This is mere surmise, says Colonel Churchward, for the records clearly state that the Land of Mu lay to the west of America in the Pacific, and not to the east in the Atlantic, which was the locality of Atlantis. And continuing his criticism of his rivals, the colonel insists that Dr Le Plongeon was wrong, because he placed Mu in Central America, forgetting entirely that all the records state quite categorically that the 'Lands of the West' were destroyed and submerged while Central America is to this day unsubmerged. 'This,' says Colonel Churchward, 'is as plausible as saying that a certain man is dead while he is arguing some point with you.' The logic here is perhaps a little difficult to follow, but the colonel is manifestly dismissing his predecessors, the doctors Schliemann and Le Plongeon, as impostors.

Those interested in the occult investigations into the Atlantis myth, can, then, decide for themselves which is most convincing, the Mu of Le Plongeon, Schliemann, or Churchward; and the claims of Mu must, in turn, be weighed against those of Lemuria as advocated by Steiner, Madame Blavatsky, and Scott-Elliott. Nor must the various locations of Atlantis itself be overlooked, even though they range from the Arctic Circle almost down to the Equator and from the West Indies to the Japanese chain of islands.

The search is an exciting one and for those with the time and access to a large library, it could easily become a challenging hobby, like finding the key to the Etruscan language, or the answer to the medieval riddle of how many angels could cluster on the head of a pin. For those who prefer their history to be more conventional on the other hand, the following chapter presents the findings of the professional historians.

## 4: THE SOLUTION OF THE SCHOLARS

To the majority of scholars who base their writing and interpretation of history on fact – or, failing that, on probability – the difficulty of Plato's Atlantis has been firstly, the *chronology* and secondly, the *geography* of the lost island. Setting the time of its destruction back 9,000 years from Solon's visit to Egypt in about 590 BC, we arrive at a date of *c.* 9,590 BC. As we have already seen, it is quite impossible for any inhabitants of this planet at that epoch to have reached the advanced stage of civilization which Plato ascribes to the Atlanteans. The philosopher even credits them with the art of writing, whereas it is now pretty well established that letters, as distinct from pictograms, first appear somewhere around 3,000 BC as an invention of the Sumerians. Plato's dating, then, for various factual reasons, cannot be right.

Secondly, the location of Atlantis as lying beyond the Pillars of Hercules. Here, too, objective science is sceptical. Admittedly at one time it was thought that the Atlantic Ridge which is known to run roughly on a north-south axis from Iceland down through the Azores and Tristan da Cunha to the South Atlantic was the spine of a submerged land mass, the discovery of which was hailed as positive proof of the authenticity of Plato's location for Atlantis. There followed a number of rather vague rumours about larval deposits on this ridge, suggesting that the land had been overwhelmed by volcanic and seismic disturbances. On the basis of these geographical data, some Atlantologists who clung fervently to the declared location beyond the Pillars and therefore in the Atlantic postulated the hypothesis that the original land mass had during the Late Tertiary time (20,000 BC) broken into two remnants, vestiges of which are seen today in the islands off the coasts of Spain and Africa, and, in the western Atlantic, in the West Indian archipelago. The former remnant constituted the islands of Atlantis; the latter, those of Antillia.

Unfortunately for this attractive theory, geologists now tend to reverse the process, as it were, asserting that the Atlantic Ridge was forced *upward* from the ocean floor and is not the spine of a continent that sank below the waves. If this is so – and one should again note what an acute observer once remarked – that you can prove anything you want with geology – all physical evidence that there was a kingdom of Atlantis such as Plato describes beyond the Pillars of Hercules is nullified.

There is also another important consideration to be taken into account as regards the location of the lost world. Plato's knowledge of geography beyond the confines of the eastern and central Mediterranean was minimal: he had only the vaguest idea of what lay beyond Carthage, let alone the Straits of Gibraltar. The ocean was actually, for him, rather like 'outer space' to us. He called it, incidentally, not the Atlantic but the Sea of Atlas. The name is derived from the giant Atlas who was forced to support the heavens on his head and hands, which he did from his fixed position *inside* the Straits. In other words, Plato seems to have accepted the Sea of Atlas as a region sufficiently far away and sufficiently mysterious to accord with the sensational nature of his report.

Those students of Atlantis, therefore, who do not

feel bound by the chronological and geographical details are able to approach the report in a less restricted
manner. One such inspired person was a young professor of Queen's University, Belfast, who, like Michael
Ventris, the decipherer of Linear B, died young. K. T.
Frost was killed in action in the First World War and
so never lived to develop the brilliant thesis he first advanced as early as 1909.[30] His thesis was, in brief, that
the story the Egyptian priests told to Solon – the story
that was eventually told to Socrates and then published
by Plato – was a typical mixture of fact and legend
which actually described a positive historic event
which had been passed down not in written words but
by means of folk-tales. That memorable event was the
destruction of the Minoan civilization by fire and
water some time around or after 1,500 BC.

What does Frost's thesis mean, then, in terms of
Plato's Atlantis myth?

It means first of all that what the Egyptian priests
called Atlantis (if this was the name of the 'Lost Island'
which they actually gave to Solon) was really Crete.
And it means in the second place that the date which
they mention for this catastrophic event referred to
some period in the remote past – not to the round figure of 9,000 years, but to a long, long time ago. It is
as though the teller of a tale prefaced his story with
some such words as 'once upon a time thousands of
years ago. . . .' To Solon, Socrates, Plato and his fellow
Athenians, both the Minoan civilization and the mil-
lennial time-scale were equally obscure, rather like the
ancient Britons to us; or, we could say, they knew as

little about the Cretan empire in 1,500 BC as we know about pre-Sumerian culture.

Yet Professor Frost had noticed certain significant details in Plato's account which suddenly made sense, as it were, as a result of the sensational findings of Sir Arthur Evans who had begun work at Knossos in 1900. Frost noticed, for instance, that Crete was 'the centre of a great empire whose trade and influence extended from the North Adriatic to Egypt and from Sicily to Syria' – a fact which corresponds to the description of Atlantis which 'had such an amount of wealth as was never before possessed by kings or potentates, and is not likely ever to be again . . . for because of the greatness of their empire, many things were brought to them from foreign countries, and the island itself provided most of what was required by them for the uses of life'.

He remembered, too, that 'strange stories must have floated around the Levant of vast bewildering palaces, of sports and dances, and above all of the bull-fight. . . . The Minoan realm must have seemed a separate continent with a genius of its own.' Compare this bull ritual of Crete with the Egyptian priests' long references to what went on in the Temple of Poseidon on Atlantis where 'bulls had range of the temple and were hunted without weapons, and the bull which was caught was led up to the altar and sacrificed'.

Frost then refers to Crete as the great maritime power of the Mediterranean, though at this point he did not have available the all-important evidence of Professor Spyridon Marinatos, the Director of the

Greek Archaeological Service, let alone the 'new' history of the Minoan civilization as it has been written on the basis of the brilliant work of archaeologists like Professor Carl Blegen and cryptologists like Michael Ventris and John Chadwick. Unaware of the theory that Crete was mortally damaged by volcanic eruptions and that its empire was proto-Hellenic, Frost fell back on the traditional belief that Knossos and the other Cretan cities were destroyed by those Bronze Age invaders who swept out of the north burning and looting their way across Greece, the Aegean islands, the Near East, and so down to Egypt – the mysterious Mitanni, Hittites, and Hyksoi.

Even so, the parallelism between the invasion of Plato's Atlanteans of Europe and Libya (meaning in classical terms North Africa from the Atlantic seaboard to the frontiers of Egypt) and the incursions by the North People into Africa and so down to Egypt is striking. The Atlanteans were supposed to have invaded around 9,600 BC, which, as we have seen, is a mythical or 'non-date' in terms of factual history. The Hyksoi reached Egypt perhaps as early as 2,500 BC. We can see how such remote dates could easily become confused in the folk-memory, but what Professor Frost so perceptively deduced was that neither precise dates nor exact locations were as important as the memory of (a) a powerful empire which existed across the sea from Egypt; and (b) the invasion of the Near East by an unknown people; and (c) the eventual destruction of the empire 'by violent earthquakes and floods in a single day and night of misfortune'.

When the clues are examined in this context – that is, the context of history rather than of mythology – the argument for Atlantis equals Crete seemed to the young classics professor at Queen's University, Belfast, to be almost conclusive.

It is important to remember that Frost's thinking on the subject was not cluttered up by a vast mass of vague mythological, geological, and anthropological impedimenta which students of Plato's story had accumulated since 17th-century scholars like Dr Olof Rudbeck placed Atlantis in his native country of Sweden. Probably Frost had read, or dipped into, Ignatius Donnelly's *Atlantis*, though it is unlikely that he would have wasted much time on the pseudo-scientific theories of Dr Augustus Le Plongeon or the *Secret Doctrine* of Madame Blavatsky. Together with all the career-classicists led by Professor Jowett, the greatest of British authorities on Plato, Frost was probably somewhat contemptuous of evidence derived from documents which were 'written in the original language of mankind' and concealed in the archives of unnamed Indian temples. In contrast, his specialized knowledge in the ancient Greek language, literature, and history, combined with the extraordinary discoveries of Sir Arthur Evans at Knossos, provided him with both actual *facts* and rational deductions with which to speculate. In this spirit, characteristic of the highest principles of scholarship, he set forth his thesis for the consideration of serious students. It is, perhaps, symbolic of the nature of human intelligence that his brilliant subjective analysis was disregarded in preference for such fictions as the Land of Mu and such occult fantasies as men fifteen feet high with an eye in the back of their head.

What K. T. Frost had done, then, was to re-appraise Plato's myth in the logical manner of a scientist who tries to separate the probable from the impossible. What is probable is susceptible to eventual proof; the impossible can be left to the fantasists. This, of course, is where the searchers for Atlantis part company.

Yet Frost's thesis, beautifully argued though it was, remained a side issue of Atlantology for over thirty years, of interest only to a few classical historians and archaeologists. One of this group, Professor Marinatos, himself a Greek, had the advantage of being able to examine the whole area of the Minoan–Mycenean complex *in situ*, in particular the islands adjacent to Crete. He noted that Greek tradition, often recorded in the guise of legends by the classical writers, coincided with, even if it did not confirm, the almost universal folk-memory of a cataclysmic flood, best known to the Christian world in the Old Testament account of the Deluge. When the Babylonian, Egyptian, and ancient Greek writings all described similar catastrophes, no one could doubt that such a catastrophe had overtaken the ancient world, though evidently at different times and in different places.

In Greek literature the story of the flood is associated with Deucalion and his ark in which he saved himself together with his wife after floating for nine days and nine nights on the waters. So the memory of what had obviously been the destruction of cities, towns, forests, and fields by some violent force of nature was deep in the subconscious of the Mediterranean people, and this memory – in the more sophisticated form one would expect of the rational Greeks of Athens at its intellectual height – is certainly found in the *Timaeus* and *Critias*.

Partly as a result of the frequent references in the classical writers to inundations and to Plato's statement that Atlantis was wiped out within twenty-four hours, Professor Marinatos, with Minoan Crete in mind, turned his attention to the island of Thera, which could be the vital clue in the Frost thesis. For Thera is volcanic; it was destroyed by a violent eruption which split it into three fragments; and it lies only some seventy-five miles north of Knossos.

He first advanced his theory that Knossos and with it the Minoan civilization of Crete was overwhelmed as a result of an unprecedented violent eruption of the Thera volcano in an article in the English journal *Antiquity* in 1939.[31]

Obviously no further practical work could be done in support of the Greek professor's idea during the 1939–45 war; but when thirty years later, geologists, vulcanologists, and archaeologists cooperated to investigate the area of the Minoan empire, they found more and more evidence to show that the end came as the result of a tremendous earthquake, followed by two severe eruptions of the volcano on Thera and the inevitable tidal waves. All this happened about 1,500 BC when Crete was at the height of its power during the late Bronze

Age. Consequently, to the Egyptians 500 miles and more away from the actual scene of the disaster, the reports could only have come through in a garbled form, the main news being that a rich and powerful nation across the sea had been practically wiped out by earthquakes and floods. Whether this event was then recorded in the state archives, we have no way of knowing, though the probability is that it was, particularly if the Egyptians eventually obtained some more specific information from their agents in the Aegean. They were, after all, keenly interested in the eastern Mediterranean, especially in *Keftiu* which is now generally agreed to be their name for Crete. If it is, we have an interesting description of its location from the point of view of the pharoahs, for it is referred to in a manuscript in the phrase 'as far away as Keftiu'.

So, a thousand years after the destruction of Keftiu by seismic and tidal waves, the priests of Sais, recounting apparently from hearsay the story of that event, placed Atlantis far away from Egypt somewhere beyond the Pillars of Hercules, no longer to be seen even by the traveller since it had been wiped out despite its size and wealth. This, of course, exactly fits the condition of Crete and the Minoan cities at the time Plato wrote his account of Atlantis. The splendour that was once Knossos, the size and magnificence of the palaces at Phaistos, Mallia, and elsewhere in the islands of the Cretan Sea, were unknown to Plato or were only vaguely recalled in the Homeric epics.

What, then, are the conclusions we can draw from the

Frost–Marinatos thesis? And does the Cretan location
stand up to the scientific tests of the geologists and the
vulcanologists?

The answer to this first question is now obvious.
Plato's account of the rise and fall of Atlantis as told
to Solon by the Egyptian priests is made up of three
distinct elements: first, a hard core of facts; second, an
overlay of legend arising out of those facts; and third,
certain moral lessons which Plato as a philosopher
wished to pass on to his disciples.

Facts overlaid with myths, then. We do not need to
go back 2,000 years or more to find exactly the same
treatment of history in our own countries and within
comparatively recent times. The classical example is
the form in which the story of King Arthur of the late
Roman period has come down to us. It is a very interesting and revealing parallel to the manner in which
the story of Minos came down to the Greeks: in other
words, the hard core of historical fact has, in both cases,
become so encrusted with fanciful legends that one
can end either by not believing a word of the story or
by trying to solve the mystery by following false clues.

What K. T. Frost did, then, was to separate what
seemed to be credible in Plato's account from what was
manifestly impossible and also from what was evidently
the 'moral' of the story. Careful readers of the relevant
passages in the *Timaeus* and *Critias* can sort out these
elements for themselves without much difficulty. An
example of what is credible – that is, based on probable
fact – is the description of the temple of Poseidon in
which the sacrificial bulls were kept and hunted. The

poetic accounts of Minos and the Minotaur were always considered legendary, belonging with the sometimes far-fetched and sometimes even ridiculous annals of the gods and their amours. But the excavations at Knossos and especially the famous frescoes of the bull-dancers proved that the bull cult in honour of Poseidon did exist in Crete as Plato describes it as existing in Atlantis.

So much for probable fact. An example of the purely mythological element is the typically Greek account of the origin of the Atlanteans – Poseidon begetting children by a mortal woman, her children in turn begetting offspring by other gods or godlings, and the sons of these unions becoming the kings of cities and provinces. Such, of course, was the explanation and justification of the theory of the divine right of kings, a fertile field for mythologists, but of small interest to the historian.

And an example of Plato's desire to point up the moral of his Atlantis story is his ending: at least the ending as far as he wrote it, because either he did not live to complete the *Critias* dialogue which breaks off in mid-sentence, or the rest of the manuscript was lost. But the ending as far as we have it is 'philosophical': it asserts that the Atlanteans who began by 'despising everything but virtue' grew slowly debased as the divine portion of their nature 'became diluted too often and too much with the mortal admixture and the human nature got the upper hand'. In other words, we have here the Platonic theory of the Fall of Man which, in contrast to the Hebrew version which ascribes that Fall to man's desire for knowledge, blames it on his growing materialism. 'They were becoming tainted with unrighteous ambition and power.'

So much, then, for the philosophical content of Plato's account of Atlantis. But we are concerned with the hard core of facts which brings us back again to Crete and to the volcanic island of Thera. The island is still an extremely active volcano which erupted strongly in 1925–6 and again during 1938–41. It has, in fact, been erupting continually for thousands of years, a series of great explosions occurring around 1,500 BC and reaching their climax from thirty to fifty years later when Crete was finally overwhelmed by the culminating disaster.

It is not proposed to analyse here all the scientific and technical evidence which the supporters of the Frost–Marinatos theory have put forward to show that the Minoan Empire of Crete was largely destroyed by the constant earthquakes and tidal waves associated with the devastating eruptions of Thera fifteen centuries before our era. Interested students will find references to the principal contributions in the Bibliography. Suffice it to say that the theory has received formidable support from the work of seismologists on the one hand and archaeologists on the other. The former have shown that the eruptions at Thera are almost paralleled by those at Krakatoa some 3,200 years later. Krakatoa is an island of the Malay Peninsula, lying between Sumatra, Java, and Borneo. It literally exploded in 1883 and was reduced to almost one-third of its former size. Its tremendous eruption combined with fifty-foot-high tidal waves caused the deaths of some 40,000 people, the destruction of nearly 300 towns and villages, the loss of hundreds of ships and small boats hurled inland thirty feet above sea level, and the inundation of tens of thousand of acres of plantations and forests. Significantly the blast waves from the explosion caused the collapse of buildings one hundred miles away from Krakatoa. Crete is only some seventy miles south of Thera and its buildings in Minoan times were built largely of sun-dried mud bricks.

The archaeologists have found considerable evidence on Thera of the effects of the eruptions in excavations which began in the 1860s and have been continued on and off up to the present; Minoan-style buildings have been found under thick banks of pumice laid down by the explosions of 1500–1470 BC. In fact, the Minoan civilization could be said to have been re-discovered first in 1870 when two French archaeologists opened up a house near Akrotiri in the south-west corner of Thera proper and found a passage whose plastered walls were decorated with frescoes in blood-red, pale yellow, dark brown, and brilliant blue – the colours we associate with the frescoes of the palace of Knossos on Crete found thirty years later by Sir Arthur Evans. So it was clear by 1870 that there had been on the island of Thera a civilized and highly artistic people whose culture – paintings, pottery, jewels, and so forth – was pre-Hellenic. Clearly, too, this civilization had been destroyed by the volcano which was still erupting as the archaeologists excavated. In the latest excavations conducted by Professor Marinatos and Emily Vermeule other houses have been uncovered and rich finds of sherds and other artefacts revealed. It is now beginning to be thought that Thera before the eruptions of 1,500 BC was an island-colony of Crete, no doubt with a Cretan governor. Future excavations may unearth this ruler's palace, though we cannot expect the rapid results that archaeologists achieved a century ago when the search was concentrated mainly on finding artefacts for museums, like the collection of pottery now housed in the French School of Archaeology at Athens. Today the excavators are especially mindful of how fabrics and frescoes can crumble and disintegrate on exposure to the air after having been buried for three and a half thousand years under vast banks of ash and pumice.

The probability that Thera was a Minoan colony becomes almost certain in the light of the other colonies and bases which Crete established through the Aegean. So there is no doubt that the historian Thucydides, writing in the 4th century BC, was stating historical fact when he stated that Minos acquired a fleet, cleared the Greek seas of pirates, and established an overseas empire with his sons as rulers. This empire, ruled from the palace at Knossos, lasted 600 years. By about 1,470 BC it appears to have collapsed, not only in the heartland of Crete but throughout its island colonies. One theory was that it was destroyed by the North Men during their migrations southwards in search of land and loot; another, that Cretan hegemony collapsed as a result of civil wars; and still a third, that the Cretans voluntarily renounced their suzerainty to the now powerful Mycenaeans.

It is, of course, best left to the experts to argue the pros and cons of the different explanations for the *sudden* eclipse of Crete and the rapid decline of the Minoan cultural dominance. It is worth remembering, however, that Cretan dominance of the seas was so strong that the possibility of the empire having been destroyed by invasion is unlikely: no sizeable armada would have been able to reach the island in sufficient strength to destroy all the cities and palaces of the imperial homeland.

Hence the alternative theory for the collapse of the great and powerful Minoan empire – the sudden and swift destruction of the kingdom by the violent eruptions on Thera, the accompanying earthquakes, and the subsequent tidal waves. Moreover, this terrible cataclysm did not only destroy towns, harbours, palaces, and villas, but undoubtedly wrecked the naval bases in adjacent islands like Thera, with the total loss of the fleets which were anchored there. Crete was thus left exposed to both the hostile Greeks and the prowling pirates, the former always eager to end the sending of tribute to Minos in the form of well-born youths and maidens for sacrifice in the Temple of Poseidon; the latter ever ready to pounce on undefended cities in search of loot.

And so we come back to Plato's account of the fall of Atlantis – the island-kingdom far distant from Egypt; an empire of the sea, guarded by its great fleets; the centre of the worship of Poseidon and the bull cult; a land of magnificent palaces and immense wealth – a country of the remote past which was overthrown in a single day and night of violent earthquakes and floods; an island that disappeared in the depths of the sea. Substitute the name Crete for Atlantis, disregard the fabulous time-scale and the location, and the philosopher's story begins to read not, it is true, like an official report of a disaster, but quite like Homer's poeticized account of the Fall of Troy. In other words, Plato has given us the essence, if not the facts, of an actual historical event.

# Part Two

## Lost Lands of the East

### 5: THE GARDEN OF EDEN

THE reader is now in a position to judge for himself the findings of the two schools of Atlantologists, the scientists on the one hand, the mystics on the other. What, it is hoped, has also emerged from this survey is the importance of our attitude and approach to a whole area of historical inquiry which the more sceptical or opinionated scholars have often dismissed as futile – as Dr Jowett, for instance, dismissed the Atlantis myth of Plato.

In brief, the least we can learn from the enormous and admittedly sometimes bizarre literature on the subject of lost lands is that the final word has not yet been spoken and that every generation of inquirers has something suggestive, if not conclusive, to offer. True, one has the impression that there is little more in the way of factual evidence to submit now that the finest scholars have brought every aid of science to bear upon the problem of Atlantis. All future speculation concerning Plato's report will either have to confirm the Minoan theory or produce another equally convincing.

The 'inspirational' type of speculation seems now to have had its day, though it may still appeal to those who prefer a mystical to a rational view of man's history.

Yet there still remain a number of unsolved mysteries in this twilight area of legend, and some of the more common of these folk-memories will be considered in the second part of this survey. The point is that whereas all of them might have been dismissed as 'old wives' tales' during the period when the rather frantic search for Atlantis incited the scorn of professional scholars, we would do well to suspend judgment now that the Platonic myth has been shown to have a firm foundation in historical fact. In other words, myths, however fantastic they may seem to us, may, and probably do, have their origin in actual events or experiences. They cannot, therefore, be explained away as the poetic fictions of some ancient story-teller, as we ought now to know since Schliemann discovered the Troy of Homer and the German archaeologist Robert Koldewey found the site of Nebuchadnezzar's Hanging Gardens of Babylon.

The myth of the Garden of Eden is an example. It was once accepted as 'gospel truth', of course, by every Christian, since the Bible was held to be the word of God and not the historical annals of the Jews. Then, in the mid-19th century, the sceptics, notably a number of German scholars of formidable erudition, questioned with powerful arguments the historicity of the Old Testament and, with the evidence of anthropology, geology, and kindred disciplines, demonstrated

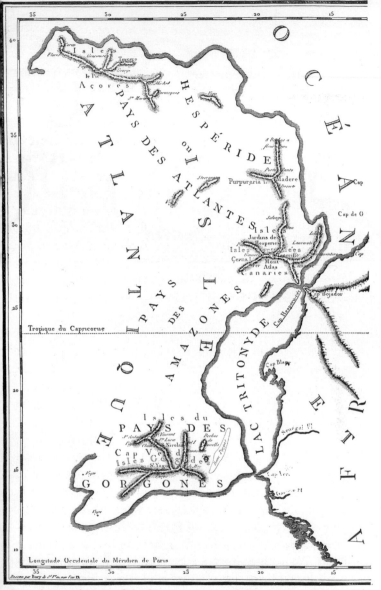

. A conjectural map of the lost continent of Atlantis taken from Bory
St Vincent's *Sur Les Canaries*. Drawn in 1803, the map shows Atlantis
situated west of the Moroccan coast, and also the country of the
Amazons.

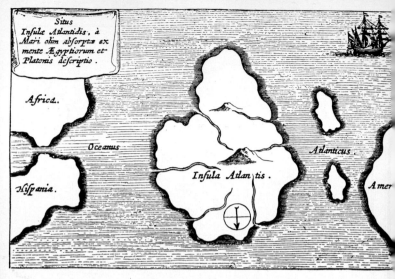

2. *Above*. A map of Atlantis shown as equidistant between Ameri
and Africa, by the 17th-century scholar, Athanāsius Kircher.

3. *Opposite*. An 18th-century map records traces of what might b
Atlantis between the coasts of Brazil and Africa, perhaps the shoa
of which Plato wrote. From the town of Rio Grande, itself situated c
a sandy peninsula, the cartographer points out the sandbanks acro
the ocean to the coast of Sierra Leone, and the diagram beneath shov
a cut-away section of the underwater line between the two continent

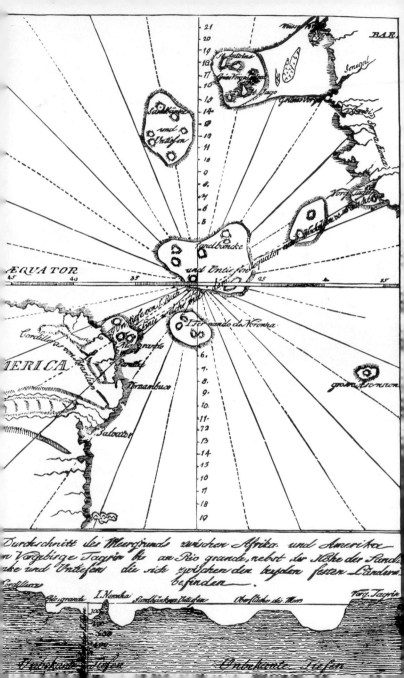

BAR.

Senegal

Bandés Sara kénér

AEQUATOR

AEQUATOR

Vorg. Jagrin

45 40 35 30 25 20 15

Cordillera von Brasilien

AMERICA

I. Fernando da Noronha

Rio grande

Fernambuco

S. Salvador

grobe Sonnen

Durchschnitt des Meergrunds zwischen Afrika und Amerika
in Vorgebirge Jagrin bis an Rio grande, nebst der Höhe der Sand-
bäncke und Untiefen die sich zwischen den beyden festen Ländern
befinden.

Cordillera                                                              Vorg. Jagrin
Rio grande   I. Noronha   Sandbäncken Untiefen   Oberfläche des Meers

Bekannte Tiefen                    Unbekannte Tiefen

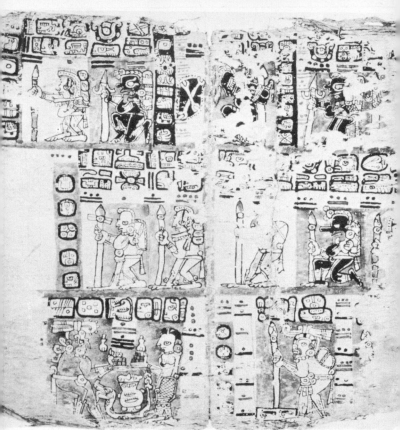

4. A page from the Mayan
manuscript, the Troano
Codex, which recounts the
destruction of Mu – the real
name, according to Dr Le
Plongeon, of Atlantis.

5. The so-called Cross of Atlantis, an
ancient symbol allegedly showing the
three concentric walls of the capital city
and the great waterway from the south.

Because mencion is made in the tenth verse of this seconde chapter of the riuer that watered the garden, we muste note that Euphrates and Tygris called in Hebrewe, Perath and Hiddekel, were called but one riuer where they ioyned together, els they had sure heades: that is, two at their springs, & two where they fel into the Persian sea. In this cowntrey and moste plentiful land Adam dwelt, and this was called Paradise: that is, a garden of pleasure, because of the frutefulnes and abundance thereof. And whereas it is said that Pishon compasseth the land of Hauilah, it is meant of Tygris, which in some place, as it passed by diuers places, was called by sundry names, as some time Diglitto, in other places Pasitygris, & of some Thasin or Pishon. Likewise Euphrates towarde the cowntrey of Cush or Ethiopia, or Arabia was called Gihon. So that Tygris and Euphrates (which were but two riuers, and some time when they ioyned together, were called after one name) were according to diuers places called by these foure names so that they might seme to haue bene foure diuers riuers.

6. A map of the Garden of Eden taken from the Book of Genesis in the Geneva or 'Breeches' Bible of 1560, showing its supposed situation and the great rivers which divide it.

5378 - ROMA - Il Paradiso terrestre - Breughel - Gall. Doria - Anderson

7 and 8. Two differing conceptions of the Garden of Eden and it
geography. The engraving below shows lush exotic countryside with
snow-capped mountains in the distance, while the Breughel painting
above shows the Creation amidst unmistakably European forest-land

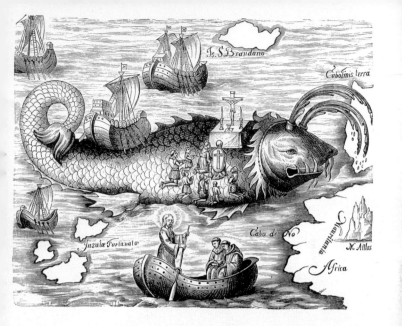

9 and 10. Irish monks, like St Brendan, were going on sea pilgrimages from the 5th century onwards; these two illustrations show some of the wonders which the saint and his companions encountered during their famous voyage, notably the amiable whale on which they landed, mistaking it for a small island.

11. In a painting by Archer, we see King Arthur nearing death mourned by the four queens, before he is taken to Avalon, 'the island to the west'.

that the story of Creation and of the Garden of Eden was merely an ancient Jewish story-teller's attempt to explain the origin of the world and of mankind. From this time on, it would be true to say that few educated people accepted the Biblical version of the Creation or the existence of a Garden of Eden. But we know now that they may well have been too hasty in denying any validity to the latter myth, for as a result of the discovery of the great libraries of the Assyrian kings, the story of the Garden of Eden, of the Flood, and of many other 'impossible' events recounted in the Old Testament are now seen to have their origin in some episode that actually took place before written records were kept. Such episodes had been passed down from generation to generation and so had become legends.

Perhaps no myth has ever intrigued more men than that of the Garden of Eden where the human race is supposed to have originated. The description of this Garden in the second chapter of Genesis is short, but extremely evocative: painters and poets have been able to depict this earthly paradise for us in all its salient details. The focus of the picture, of course, is the Tree of Knowledge in which the serpent hides in order to tempt Eve to eat of the fruit which, incidentally, is nowhere called an apple. And ever since the Bible became the source book of Christian ethics, philosophers have pondered the symbolism of the serpent, the Tree of Knowledge, the Fall of Man, and the culpability of Woman for having us expelled from that delightful retreat. More practical-minded scholars, in

the meantime, have sought for the actual location of
the Garden of Eden, using the clues that are given in
Genesis, for it would be most fascinating to see the
place where we all began.

Taking the name Eden first. The Hebrew word
appears to be cognate with the Accadian EDINU,
meaning a flat plain, or steppe. At the same time, a
similar Hebrew word has the connotation of 'pleasure'
or 'delight'and so the Greek translation for the Hebrew
phrase Garden of Eden became – παράδεισος τῆς
τρυφῆς : literally, 'a delightful woodland retreat',
or 'sylvan paradise'. Originally, however, Eden must
have been an oasis in the desert, well wooded and
watered as described in Genesis; for the celebrated
second chapter describes the river which made the
area fertile as dividing into four streams after it left
the Garden. These branches are named as:

1. Pishon
2. Gihon
3. Hiddekel
4. Euphrates

The third of these rivers is translated into Greek as
the Tigris, which is the obvious nomenclature since the
Bible says that Hiddekel 'goeth in front of Assyria'.
By 'Assyria' Persia is probably meant, since all geography in ancient time was imprecise. The location of
the first and second rivers is very controversial, and all
we can say is that the early Jewish and Christian commentators believed that Pishon was the Ganges and
Gihon the Nile. In other words, the Biblical account of

the creation of the world and the origin of man assumed that the four great rivers of the world, as known to the primitive Semites of the Middle East – the Tigris, Euphrates, Ganges, and Nile – became a single stream encircling the central land mass. The concept of a river, or ocean, which flowed round the earth is, in fact, basic to nearly all geography, both Semitic and Greek, up to the early Middle Ages.

Starting with some extremely vague clues as to the whereabouts of Eden, searchers have located the Garden all over the world, from the North Pole to Australia, though usually these sites have been chosen on the basis of 'astral guidance', which we saw was the method used by the Theosophists and other occultists to locate Atlantis. As for the early historians and geographers, notably Josephus (1st century AD) and Cosmas Indicopleustes (6th century AD), they, too, relied on intuition and placed Eden in the extreme northwest, as far away as the Altai Mountains of northern Asia. Their choice was not based, of course, on any physical evidence, but on pure speculation.

Modern geographers, on the other hand, have limited the area in which the Garden could possibly have been to the alluvial plains between the Two Rivers: that is, to the Land of Sumer in Lower Mesopotamia, the site of the world's first civilization. Here originated many of the creation-myths and a great deal of the religious history of the Semites, including that of the Babylonians, Assyrians, and Jews. The concept of the Garden of Eden is undoubtedly Sumero-Babylonian in origin, as the role played by the serpent and the cherubim indicate. The serpent, or dragon, became an important symbol in the Babylonian story of creation and was to become the mascot, as it were, of the chief god Marduk. Both the dragon and the cherubim were used as religious decorations on Assyrio-Babylonian temples, the former beast best seen in the charming coloured tiles of the famous Ishtar Gate of Babylon; and the latter in the immense man-headed winged bulls and lions which kept guard at the entrance to the sacred shrines.

Undoubtedly the myth of an earthly paradise arose as a result of the oases of lush greenery found in an otherwise vast desert land, for the Two Rivers, the Euphrates and the Tigris, flow through one of the most arid regions of the world, with the Syrian Desert to the west, the Arabian Desert to the south, and eroded mountains to the north and east. In the middle of this barren landscape where survival has always been so difficult for man and beast alike lies the green alluvial plain of Mesopotamia, abounding in gardens, palm groves, shady trees, and, above all, pools of water. To the desert-dwellers, this was Paradise.

Perhaps, therefore, the most likely site for the Garden of Eden is somewhere in ancient Babylonia where the country was once far more luxuriant than it is today, since the Babylonian kings were particularly conscientious about keeping the canals and irrigation channels in working order, as their inscriptions proudly announce. Hence, if two of the rivers mentioned in Genesis are accepted as the Euphrates and Tigris, the other two, Pishon and Gihon, may be the

Hebrew names for two of the great canals which joined the two main arteries. However, it is difficult to be more precise, since the Euphrates and Tigris have changed their course radically since the second millennium BC, and the old canal system of the Sumero-Babylonian empires has collapsed completely. Otherwise the explorer could, perhaps, find some clue in the region where the Sumerian city of Eridu once stood near the mouth of the Euphrates, which at the epoch we are speaking of flowed directly into the Persian Gulf. Eridu was known as 'the good city'; or, in other words, a holy place on account of the shrine of the god Tammuz who dwelt in the shade of a sacred palm tree, while the goddess Bahu had her couch in the foliage of the same tree. This scene is frequently depicted in Accadian sculptures, while a cylinder seal, now in the British Museum, represents two figures, a male and a female, seated on opposite sides of a tree with hands stretched toward it. Behind the woman is an upright snake. Clearly, then, the Tree, the Snake, and the primeval Man and Woman are a Sumero-Babylonian creation myth which was conceivably borrowed by the early Jewish chroniclers.

The Moslems, too, accept the story of the Garden of Eden, as they do all of the Old Testament myths, but their true Paradise is a celestial, not an earthly, abode, and is located in the regions of the Beyond where dwell the 'Companions of the Night'. This Moslem heaven in other words, is a Garden in the Persian sense: specifically, a park dotted about with pavilions where the houris are housed, with leaping fountains, streams of living water, of milk, wine, and honey, fountains scented with camphor or ginger, shady valleys, all sorts of delicious fruits, and exquisite banquets served in priceless vessels by youths who never grow old. The location of this Garden is under the throne of God above the highest heaven and is therefore to be distinguished from the Garden of Adam, which was an earthly paradise. The Old Testament site of Eden is placed by the Arabs at the confluence of the Euphrates and the Tigris – at the village of Al Qurnah, forty miles north-west of Basra. Here they will point out the original Tree of Knowledge in whose trunk they say lives a serpent, friendly to believers, but able to vanish into thin air as an unbeliever approaches. It reminds one of the story pilgrims used to tell about the saint buried at St Catherine's monastery on Sinai who would reach out from his coffin to shake hands with the faithful but would refuse to salute doubters altogether.

## The Hesperides

The legends of other nations, too, have their Gardens of Eden, and they all suggest, as the Hebrew version suggests, that they originated in some vague folk-memory of a beautiful landscape where men lived in peace and innocence, close to nature and the gods. Such a paradise was the Greek Hesperides, or the Garden of the Daughters of the Evening, located according to some authorities in Arcady, that isolated valley of southern Greece whose inhabitants were simple herdsmen and hunters. Untroubled by the problems of civilization, these unsophisticated children of nature worshipped Pan, the most attractive of all the nature-gods. It is his pipes which are heard on the hillside; and it is under his protection that not only the flocks and herds, but all animals, wild as well as domesticated, flourish and increase. The theme of man's innocence is, we see, basic to both the Hebrew and the Greek myth, though the ancient Jewish moralists introduced an element which is not present in Greek thinking: namely, the concept of original sin. As a result of the stern punishment meted out to man for eating of the Tree of Knowledge, nobody has ever expected to return to Eden, whereas the Greeks, and later the Romans, continued to search for their lost paradise, which they variously called Arcady, the Gardens of the Hesperides, the Elysian Fields, and the Islands of the Blest. Homer believed in some such happy land and describes it as a place where 'the life of mortals is most easy, and there is no snow or winter, nor much rain, but the Ocean is ever sending up cool breezes to refresh men'. In fact there came a time when men really thought that this earthly paradise had been discovered: that the Islands of the Blest, or the Fortunate Islands, as the Romans called them, actually existed: had been visited by explorers; and were ready to be set down on the maps.

The rumour probably originated in the Mediterranean seaports frequented by the Phoenician and Carthaginian merchantmen. The sea captains of Carthage had been sailing out into the Atlantic for centuries, and they had undoubtedly discovered by the 1st century BC islands which answered the description of Homer's idealized country. But the Punic mariners never gave away any information of their trading routes if they could help it, which is partly the reason why they had a monopoly on maritime commerce beyond the Pillars of Hercules. But after the total annihilation of Carthage, some of the secrets of their discoveries must have been learnt by the Romans whose fleets now commanded the seas, for we hear of the Roman general Quintus Sertorius planning in 82 BC to send a naval expedition to find the Fortunate Isles which certain sailors claimed to have actually visited. They lay, said these mariners, 1,000 miles to the west of Cadiz, which suggests the Azores whose climate is certainly all that Homer ascribes to the Fortunate Isles. But it is more likely that the Canaries, which lie some 600 miles to the south-southwest of Cadiz, are the islands which the Cathaginians had discovered during the famous voyage of exploration by Hanno down the west coast of Africa; for it was the Canary Islands which later geographers like Ptolemy were able to name and locate with some exactness.

This deep-seated belief in an earthly paradise, whether it was called the Garden of the Hesperides, Arcady, the Fortunate Isles, or the Elysian Fields is characteristic of classical mythology, and the same Utopian dream will be found in the Celtic world of northern Europe. The names of these lost and once sacred places vary from country to country and from age to age, but the underlying theme is always the same – the happy and tranquil life spent in beautiful surroundings where neither work nor strife is necessary for survival. The Hebrew Garden of Eden, the Greek Isles of the Blest, the Welsh Avalon, the Cornish Lyonnesse, the Breton City of Ys, the Portuguese Antilia are all derived from the same longings of men for an ideal world. All, too, seem to embody, deep under the layers of myth, some imperfectly remembered event in history, usually the disappearance of an island or continent long ago; and as the old people told the story of this catastrophe to their children, the vanished country became more and more desirable as it receded into the mists of time.

## 6: THE COUNTRY OF THE QUEEN OF SHEBA

WHO actually was the Queen of Sheba, that mysterious Oriental princess who crossed the Syrian desert to visit King Solomon? Scholars have tried to solve the enigma of her nationality, and travellers have searched for her country. But no one has yet succeeded in identifying this royal lady who, the Bible tells us, came to Jerusalem 'with a very great train, with camels that bare spices, and very much gold, and precious stones'. And no one has yet found the country from which she came.

The original story in the First Book of Kings (ch. x, 1–13) states that the Queen came to see Solomon because she had heard so much about his wisdom; and after she had questioned him, departed, saying, 'It was a true report that I heard in my own land of thy acts and thy wisdom'.

We learn too, that the two monarchs exchanged gifts,

Solomon receiving 120 talents of gold and a great quantity of spices; and the Queen 'all her desire, whatsoever she asked'.

On the basis of these few facts, an extensive mythology has grown up around the shadowy figure of the Queen of Sheba, especially in Arabia and Ethiopia, both of which countries claim the princess as their own. For a royal lady who travelled in such style strongly appealed to the Oriental imagination. And, in addition, a king like Solomon who was rich, wise, generous, God-fearing, and the master of a splendid harem was the ideal monarch. It was only right and proper that two such remarkable people should come together.

But the Biblical account of the famous queen ends with the short reference to her in the Old Testament: there is no mention of her in any other historical context, though, as we shall see, a whole literature grew up around her figure, so that she has become perhaps the most famous queen in history. But the whereabouts of her kingdom, which was so rich in gold, precious stones, perfumes, and incense, remains a mystery despite the several almost convincing theories of the Arabian explorers. The most acceptable of these theories assumes that Sheba is the English form of Saba, the ancient Arabian kingdom which was situated in the Yemen in south-west Arabia. Saba and the Sabaeans were certainly known to ancient writers as far back as 732 BC when an Assyrian document lists Saba among the conquests of Tiglath-pileser IV. The classical geographers, too, were familiar with this Arabian kingdom whose Red Sea ports were important staging-posts on the India–Egypt sea-route, and it was as a result of that trade that Saba became rich and fairly powerful at the time of Solomon.

New impetus was given to this theory that the Queen of Sheba came from the kingdom of Saba with the discovery in the 19th century of extensive ruins and numerous inscriptions which all pointed to a high level of civilization in what is today the primitive tribal country of Yemen. Villages which now consist of a few mud dwellings and a mosque were 2,000 years and more ago large fortified towns ruled over by chieftains who called themselves kings. Such a centre of commerce and agriculture was Marib, the Mariaba of the classical geographers, the capital of ancient Saba and certainly the city where the Queen of Sheba would have her palace if we could be certain that Saba is the same as the Old Testament Sheba. Similarly, the ruins at Zafar, Sana, and Sirwak in the Yemeni highlands all point to the existence at the time of Solomon (10th century BC) to a flourishing kingdom with trade links throughout the Orient, Africa, and Mesopotamia. In these circumstances it would not be unusual for a high dignitary from Saba to travel the 1,500 miles to Jerusalem to negotiate a commercial agreement.

The fact was that, at this period, Israel was one of the most powerful states of the Near East and King Solomon one of the most successful monarchs. The cavalry wing alone of his army consisted of 12,000 horses, with 400 chariots. His foreign alliances included treaties with Egypt, Moab, Edom, and the Hittite king. His commercial alliances with the Phoenicians and

Arabians were equally profitable to him; envoys came from all over the civilized world to pay homage to this famous Israelite and, at the same time, to negotiate diplomatic and commercial treaties with him. The Queen of Sheba presumably came on some such mission on behalf of her country.

But was that country Saba in south-west Arabia? It would undoubtedly be rash to say definitely yes, for several reasons: first, there is never any mention in any of the hundreds of Sabaean inscriptions to a *queen* of Saba. All the monarchs were by tradition priest-kings such as we find in Sumer, Babylon, and Assyria. For in these primitive Semitic societies communication between the national god and the people was possible only through a man who was the ordained representative of the god on earth: namely, a pope, or royal pontiff. There were, of course, queens in the persons of the mothers and wives of kings; but the chances that there was ever a Queen of Saba in the sense of the sole reigning monarch are remote; and, even if there were, the likelihood that she herself would leave her kingdom to go as a kind of suppliant to a far country is negligible: she would certainly have sent her ambassadors.

The question of the whereabouts of Sheba is further complicated by the existence of another Saba or Seba – this one in Ethiopia and, as we find from the legends, a place which becomes quite important in the search for Sheba itself. Saba (modern Sabba) lies about one hundred miles east of Aksum, the capital of an ancient Ethiopian kingdom which was either founded by or had colonial ties with south-west Arabia. The Ethiopian Sabba, in fact, appears to have a much stronger claim to having been the home of the Queen than the Arabian Saba, for tradition recalls that it was once an important religious centre, containing the Ark of the Covenant supposed to have been brought back from Jerusalem by the Queen of Sheba's son by Solomon.

What must by this time have become clear is that the Queen of Sheba is an important personage in the legends of three literatures, Jewish, Arabic, and Ethiopic. But whereas the first of our sources as to this intriguing royal lady gives us no particulars as to her name, age, or appearance, the other two are much more informative.

In the Arab legends the Queen is called Belkis, or Bilkis and she sends a number of gifts to Solomon who, for some reason or other, is not satisfied; whereupon the Queen travels to Jerusalem herself, no doubt to placate the king. The official Moslem version of the Jewish story is found in the Koran (Sura XXVII, 15–45) which describes the Sabaean queen as 'ruling over a people who prostrate themselves to the sun'. This obvious reference to sun-worship coincides with the pantheistic religion of Yemen whose principle gods were the Venus-planet, the Moon, and the Sun (all male gods). In plain words, Belkis was a 'heathen', though this does not explain why she was so eager to visit Solomon. In fact, at first she was afraid to do so and sent instead a present of 6,000 boys and girls, all born on the same day at the same hour – a typical Arab idea of a royal gift, though rather a large number of mouths to feed even for an Oriental potentate.

In a later version of the legend, Solomon, who understood the language of the birds, sent his message to Queen Belkis by means of the hoopoe bird or lapwing who carried the letter under his wing. The message summoned Belkis to the palace at Jerusalem, a journey which was said to take seven years. But so eager was the Queen to meet the King of the Jews that she set out immediately and arrived in the record time of three years. Then the famous interview took place at which she tested Solomon's wisdom by asking him a series of riddles.

What were they? Jewish legends provide us with several examples, of which this is one: 'The Queen said, "Seven depart. Nine enter. Two pour. One drinks'. Solomon replied, 'Seven days represent the period of a woman's menstruation; nine months the period of her pregnancy; two pouring is a reference to her breasts; and one drinking, a reference to her baby".'

The Arab version of this famous meeting has a curious twist which, one must admit, adds interest and excitement to the 'plot'. It tells how the demons at Solomon's court, afraid that the king might marry Belkis, spread the rumour that the queen had hairy legs and the foot of an ass. Now in order to check these rumours, Solomon had his visitor led onto a floor of highly polished glass, and Belkis, mistaking this floor for a pool of water, lifted up her skirts and revealed her legs. Sure enough, they were covered with hair; but

Solomon in his wisdom commanded the djinn to prepare a special depilatory, for which the embarrassed queen was profoundly grateful, especially as Solomon now agreed to marry her; or rather, to add her to his collection of 300 wives, 700 concubines, and the 6,000 boys and girls she had already sent him. However, he thought enough of her to bury her in a magnificent tomb in the city of Palmyra, which stood on the northern edge of the Syrian Desert. Palmyra today is a small village of mud huts, but in Solomon's time it was an important metropolis on the East-West trade route, reaching its zenith in the Roman period during the reign of another famous Oriental queen, Zenobia.

The Ethiopians have an even more colourful legend than the Arabs, a legend that explains, incidentally, their claim that their kings are descendants from a union of Solomon with the Queen of Sheba. The story is told in an ancient Abyssinian book entitled the *Kebra-Nagasht*, or *The Glory of Kings*, in which the Queen is called Makeda ('woman of fire'), an Ethiopian princess who first heard the story of Solomon's wisdom from the merchant Tamrinn, the owner of 73 ships and 580 camels.

This man had made a special trip to Jerusalem to see Solomon, whose kindness to his servants and slaves impressed Tamrinn as much as his wisdom. Queen Makeda was also impressed, and decided to visit Solomon herself. After a long voyage, she arrived in Jerusalem where the king assigned her a palace next to his own. They saw each other every day, and after every

meeting Makeda returned to her palace 'full of delightful thoughts'. Her thoughts were no doubt stimulated
by the arrival of her daily ration: namely, 45 sacks of
flour, 10 fat barons of beef, 5 bulls, 50 sheep, an un-
specified number of goats, deer, cows, and chickens, a
barrel of *vin ordinaire*, a half-barrel of old wine, honey,
and baskets of fried locusts. It is no wonder that Makeda said to her generous host, 'I would like to be one of
your servants and to wash your feet, for I am overcome
by your handsome appearance and by your charming
conversation'. An example of Solomon's charming conversation was to explain to his guest how God produced
man from the pips of a lemon.

In the meantime (the legend tells us) Solomon had
said to himself, 'A beautiful princess has come from
the ends of the earth to see me. Who knows if it is not
God's will that she should have offspring by me?' Having decided the answer to this question was yes,
Solomon gave Makeda a great banquet on the eve of
her departure at which he plied her with highly-spiced
foods – for a reason that soon will become apparent.
Then he took her to her room and asked her to marry
him. The princess agreed, provided he promised not
to touch her. King Solomon accepted this curious condition and added one of his own: namely, that he
wouldn't touch her provided she didn't touch anything of his, including the furnishings in the room.

'What!' Makeda is reported as crying. 'I am as rich
as you. Why should I want to steal your things, if that
is what you mean?'

But that wasn't what Solomon meant at all. What

he meant was revealed during the night when Makeda, tormented by thirst, slipped out of bed, tip-toed across the room to the waterjug, picked it up, and drank. Solomon who was sleeping near by and staying awake for this eventuality immediately challenged the princess with breaking her vow. She admitted that she had done so and gracefully conceded that he was no longer bound by his oath.

The next day Queen Makeda left Jerusalem for her own capital, Aksum in northern Ethiopia, giving birth to a fine baby boy en route. And it was this son of Solomon and Makeda who, as Prince Menelik, was the first of the royal line of Ethiopian kings, officially known from that day as the 'Elect of God' and the 'Lion of Judah'.

Obviously Jewish, Arab, and Ethiopian legends have got themselves so inextricably mixed that they do not help us in our search for the actual land from which this mysterious queen came. The solution is made easier, perhaps, if the romantic associations of the relationship between the Jewish king and the Arabian queen are set aside as the inventions of desert story-tellers: the tale of the hoopoe bird, the 6,000 boys and girls, the hairy legs of the queen, the banquet, and the artful manner in which Solomon tricked his royal visitor into his bed are manifestly the stuff of which the *Thousand Nights and a Night* are composed. Such innocent yarns tell us nothing about the land of Sheba which, despite all the research which has been done on the subject, must remain 'lost'.

On the other hand, if the story is accepted as having a basis in fact, it is easier to reconstruct what might have taken place at the court of King Solomon about 950 BC and even where 'Sheba' actually was. The clue may be in the Arabic name Belkis, derived according to some scholars from the Greek παλλακίς from the Hebraised *pilegesh* according to others. Both words mean 'a concubine'. If, then, the woman who arrived at Solomon's court was part of either a gift or a tribute which included 'spices, and very much gold, and precious stones', the story begins to make sense; and, in view of the custom of the time, so do the beautiful boys and girls sent separately from the other gifts, though there could hardly have been 6,000 of them, unless they were prisoners-of-war.

Gifts, then, or tribute despatched to Jerusalem by camel caravan; and articles which could only have come from certain countries in the Middle East: all the evidence points to the kingdom of Saba which needed not only a commercial alliance with the smaller nations of the region but, above all, a military treaty in order to ward off invasions from the Assyrians. And finally, if we remember that important diplomatic alliances in Solomon's day (and for long after, for that matter) were nearly always solemnized by the king of the more powerful nation taking into his harem a princess of the royal house of the new ally, we can suppose that Belkis was a princess of the House of Saba and that her status was that of concubinage by the Jewish law even though she was called Solomon's wife in the Arabic and Ethiopic legends.

So we should perhaps, look for the palace of the 'Queen of Sheba' in the ruins which lie spread along the hillsides of Yemen. It was from here that a princess set out on the long journey northwards, never, of course, to return again to her homeland.

## 7: THE COUNTRY OF THE AMAZONS

THE idea of Amazons – that is, of a society of women who not only reject but actually defy the masculine world – has always intrigued students of psychology as it has students of history. Of course, the first question that has to be answered is whether there were any such people as the Amazons at all; and if there were, where did they come from?

The ancient writers who were nearest in time to the female warriors are quite definite about their existence, though they are not so certain about the location of their homeland; and for this reason the Country of the Amazons must be numbered among those lost lands of which we have only faint clues in myth and legend.

Any discussion of the Amazons should at once make it clear that these extraordinary women were interesting to men in classical times for quite different reasons from those which may interest us today; for neither the Greeks nor the Romans regarded them as crusaders for women's rights, political or social; nor did they automatically assume that the Amazons were lesbians who preferred the love and companionship of their own sex to that of men. These unusual women were simply a nation of warriors who attacked and sometimes conquered their neighbours, defended themselves against their enemies, and died on the battlefield like soldiers. There is, of course, no reason why such a nation of warlike women should not have existed, and there are examples of comparable Amazonian armies in modern history, notably in Dahomey in Africa. But the more civilized we become, the less we associate women with active warfare.

To the ancients, the Amazons were another semi-barbarous nation who lived on the borders of the Hellenic world, somewhere on the southern shore of the Euxine or Black Sea; or, according to later historians, in the vicinity of the Caucasus Mountains. They appear so consistently in Greek history, literature, and art from the time of Homer onwards that it is hard to deny the legend all semblance of factual truth. Indeed, we are given a fairly detailed account of their lives and activities, so that we know that they had a queen, never a king, as their ruler, a parliament of women, and an army of female soldiers. Their problem of how to keep up their numbers was easily solved; once a year they invited the men of a neighbouring tribe called the Gargareans to a festival the express purpose of which was the propagation of the race. Little else is known about these Gargareans and the annual festival of the Amazons except that the male children who resulted from this union were sent back to their fathers in some cases, or put to death in others, while the baby girls were carefully raised by their

mothers and taught at an early age to ride, hunt, and
fight, both mounted and on foot. In short, these independent women ran their own affairs without any help
or advice from men, thereby reversing the traditional
structure of classical society which was invariably
patriarchal.

The Amazonian nation appears to have flourished
from the legendary beginnings of Greek history until
the conquest of Asia by Alexander the Great, at which
time the region where the women were supposed to
have their homeland was found to contain no such
people. However, those historians who insisted on the
reality of the Amazons explained this fact away by
saying that the group had undoubtedly migrated farther to the east and north in order to avoid battle with
Macedonian king's formidable troops. But even after
the Amazons had, as it were, disappeared into the
steppes of Russia, they continued to excite the interest
of philosophers as well as of poets and painters, for
they were an exceedingly controversial ethnic group
about which the old scholars could not make up their
minds. Thus, even their name was controversial. Herodotus, for instance, says that it comes from a Scythian
word meaning 'man-killers'. Others derive it from a
Circassian word meaning 'moon-worshippers'. And
others, again, favour the Greek word $\dot{\alpha}\mu\alpha\zeta\acute{o}\varsigma$, or
'breastless', a derivation which lends credence to the
fable that the Amazons amputated or burnt off the
right breast of young girls in order that this protu-
berance might not get in the way of the bowstring and
javelin. The legend is undoubtedly false, since while

it is standard practice for men to mutilate themselves
and each other, it is unlikely that women if left to
themselves, would practise breast-excision any more
than they would tolerate clitoridectomy. Be this as it
may, the numerous statues and depictions of the
Amazons do not portray them as being deprived of
their right breast. They are not mutilated and are
shown often on horseback with a thin dress girt up for
convenience. Their arms were the bow, spear, light
ax, the crescent-shaped shield and helmet; and with
these weapons· they fought a number of battles against
the Lycians, Phrygians, Trojans, and other nations of
Asia Minor. Obviously the fact that their opponents
were women made no difference to the male armies
whom they attacked, as we can see from the paintings,
bronzes, and marble reliefs depicting their victories
and defeats: the slaughter between men and women is
just as merciless as it is between men and men. And so,
in fact, died a number of Amazonian queens, among
them Penthesilia, slain by Achilles during the Trojan
War; Hippolyte, ravished by Hercules; and Antiope,
killed by Theseus.

The first of these queens came to the aid of the
Trojans after the death of Hector, and she fought
valiantly until eventually overcome and slain by
Achilles. It seems strange to us that the greatest war-
rior of all time should have challenged a woman to
battle, as it is strange that the strongest man, namely,
Hercules, should have spent so much time and effort
to obtain the girdle of another queen, Hippolyte. The
third of the royal Amazons, Antiope, was supposed to

have been given to Theseus as a present from Hercules, to have become his wife or concubine, and to have been either killed by him, as some versions of the legend have it, or to have died fighting at his side against her fellow-countrymen who had invaded Attica.

The last of these incidents is the most important from the point of view of the historian, since no event in the prehistory of Greece appears to have been more deeply worked into the folk-memory than the invasion of Attica by the Amazons. Indeed, these armies of highly trained and well-armed women warriors who fought their way into the centre of Athens itself were no legend to the Greek historians and philosophers, Herodotus, Lysias, Plato, and Isocrates. Their march from the southern shores of the Black Sea across what today is Turkey and over the frozen Bosphorus to Greece was solemnly traced by the geographers who admitted that the women overcame all the difficulties and obstacles of this tremendous journey and still were capable of penetrating into the heart of Athens where they were finally crushed by King Theseus. Moreover, pagan archaeologists actually pointed out the evidence of the Amazons' war against Hellas in the numerous tombs, grave-mounds, and trophies, as well as the festivals and sacrifices which were associated with the Greek victory over a formidable enemy.

Where, then, was the country from which these remarkable women came? Asiatic Greece, which roughly corresponds with western Turkey, was the accepted location. The actual district was the town and plain of

Themiskyra on the river Thermodon, almost midway along the south coast of the Black Sea. But they were believed to have conquered and occupied a much wider range of territory and even to have founded cities as populous as Ephesus, Smyrna, Myrina, Paphos, and Sinope. Amazons, it was believed, were builders of the great temple of Artemis at Ephesus which was revered throughout Greece on account of the brave women who, after having been first roughly handled by Hercules and then completely defeated by Theseus, could yet find courage to play so conspicuous a part in the defence of Troy against the Grecian besiegers.

Yet despite the wealth of information about their achievements, later historians of the classical period began to doubt the existence of these women-warriors largely on the grounds that when the armies of Alexander the Great reached Themiskyra on the Thermodon in 333 BC, they found no trace of any such nation. At the same time, as if in direct contradiction to this view, another report claims that the Macedonian king was visited by a queen of the Amazons called Thalestris who wished to have a child by the invincible soldier. On the strength of this story some commentators argue that if Alexander was in the vicinity of the Amazons' country, it would have been politic for them to have appeased him in the usual oriental manner, which was to offer him a princess for his harem. And as for the apparent absence of the Amazons from their traditional seat at Themiskyra, the supporters of the legend point out that the women may by this time have migrated farther to the east. But it is perhaps significant that the deeper the penetrations of the Greeks and, later, the Romans into the Middle East, the remoter the country of the Amazons became, until we have a German scholar placing it somewhere in the Central Asian steppes from whence came those 'hairless' Mongols who periodically raided the eastern Mediterranean world. And so by the 20th century, the beautiful creatures of Greek legend had become the monsters of German scholarship.

In a word, the existence of the Amazons as historical fact remains a highly controversial subject, and perhaps the best we can do is to keep an open mind about it, as the geographer Strabo recommends. Though he was meticulously scientific in his use of evidence, Strabo has no patience with those pedants who refuse to admit the possibility that myths have a kernel of truth within them; and he is particularly severe with those sceptics who deny any historical validity to Homer's tale of Troy. In contrast, the famous Victorian historian George Grote whose *History of Greece* was written 'in the spirit of scientific criticism' states point-blank that the legend of the Amazons, *like that of the siege of Troy*, has no basis in history, but is 'merely the aggregate matter of Grecian legendary faith'. How right then, was Strabo to keep an open mind! How wrong Grote in the case of Troy! And how wrong he could be, therefore in the matter of the Amazons.

Yet our chances of ever finding any concrete evidence of this fascinating nation are admittedly slim. The Amazons were, of course, a constant source of inspira-

tion to Greek poets, orators, and mythologists, so that
we know the names of their queens, the manner in
which they educated their girl-children, the campaigns
they fought, and even the clothes they wore. But how
much of all this detail was due to fiction and how
much to fact is not known. We can only be sure that
the idea of beautiful women not only adopting manly
pursuits, but rejecting the male altogether, intrigued
those old Mediterranean pagans far more than it does
a North European today, since the latter's women have
always had much more freedom and, for that matter,
once fought alongside their menfolk. Tacitus makes
this quite clear in his description of the battle tactics
of the Germans and of the Britons when they were led
to war by their queen Boadicea. And for this reason –
the fact that the Germanic and Celtic peoples were distinguished by the belligerence of their women in
contrast to the submissiveness of the Mediterranean
and oriental women – we should perhaps look for the
country of the Amazons where the best informed
geographers of ancient times placed it: to wit, the
Sarmatian, or Central Asian, hinterland. Alternatively,
if the story of these warrior-women belongs more to
mythology than history, we can be certain that it takes
us back to that remote period of human history when
woman was the symbol of both life and death, of peace
and war, whence the palaeolithic statuettes of the so-
called Venuses; the earliest of the Mediterranean cults
centred around the concept of the Earth-Mother; and
the importance of the virgin Pallas Athene throughout
Greek history as goddess of life and war. It is interest-

ing in this respect that Athene carried a shield which is adorned with scenes from the battles of the Amazons with the Giants.

In short, the myth of the Amazons may have originated in the folk-memory of a period in history when society was matriarchal. We see the vestiges of some such system in Tacitus's description of the German tribes whose women accompanied their husbands and sons to war. We can see, too, how intriguing the idea of a truly emancipated woman was to the Greeks who, in the process of becoming civilized, had reduced their own wives and mothers to a condition of near-serfdom. Consequently the Amazons, even though they were barbarians in Greek eyes, were none the less admired as brave and free creatures, worthy of a high place in history.

## 8: THE EMPIRE OF PRESTER JOHN

A S mysterious to us today as that Country of the Amazons which occupied the attention of men throughout the classical period is the Empire of Prester John which explorers and travellers set out to find during the Middle Ages. Perhaps no other legend affected men's thinking or perhaps altered the course of history itself as surely as the belief, held by all educated men from the 12th to the 16th century, that there was such a fabulous personage as John the priest-king and a vast empire over which he ruled. Popes and kings corresponded with this unknown monarch; ambassadors were despatched to his court; and geographers marked his dominions on their maps of the world. Yet he had appeared, as it were, out of nowhere; and in the course of time, he disappeared into the twilight zone of half-forgotten myths.

The very name Prester John has an evocative sound, even though the verdict of history is that there was never any such person. But as we have seen in almost every case that we have examined, there is usually some historical fact or probability behind the often fantastic legend; behind the strange figure of Prester John looms that of the Mongol Genghis Khan, or some other tribal chieftain from the hinterland of Central Asia.

Prester John first appears on the horizon of the Western world in AD 1145 when a French bishop called Hugh brought the attention of the Pope to the existence of 'a certain John, a king and priest who dwells beyond Persia and Armenia in the uttermost East and, with all his people, is a Christian. . . . It is said that he is a lineal descendant of the Magi of whom mention is made in the Gospel and that ruling over the same peoples which they governed, he enjoys such great glory and wealth that he uses no sceptre save one of emerald. Inspired by the example of his forefathers who came to adore Christ in his manger, he had planned to go to the aid of Jerusalem, but was prevented from crossing the Tigris by the fact that the river was frozen.'

This, of course, was sensational news to Christian Europe, especially as there had always been rumours and half-facts concerning Christian colonies in India planted there by none other than the apostle Thomas. The pope and his advisers and the Catholic kings were now convinced that here was proof India was christianized as the early Christian legends claimed and that a Christian king ruled over a mighty oriental empire.

The excitement among scholars as well as prelates must have been intense as speculation about the character of the priest-king and the location of his dominions flew across Europe, and high hopes were aroused that a new and powerful ally against the Saracens had been found. One would have thought that the report about John being unable to cross the Tigris because it was frozen would have given cautious men grounds for scepticism; but Bishop Hugh was known to be an accomplished diplomat who had just come from the Middle East and knew better than any Christian what was going on there. But it seems that he did not know quite enough; for what had been going on was a tremendous battle between the Mongol prince Yeh-lü Ta-shih and the Moslem Sultan Sanjar, a battle in which the former utterly defeated the latter, a cause for Christian rejoicing in view of the difficulties the Crusaders were then having to hold their north-eastern front against Islam. But evidently Bishop Hugh's informants, either out of ignorance or in order to ingratiate themselves with him, emphasized the fact that since the victor was an enemy of Islam, he was most probably a Christian; and before long, the Chinese warlord Yeh-lü Ta-shih had become a Christian priest-king called John (*Johannes*, the Latin form of the name is not unlike the sound of Yeh-lü Ta-Shih).

Europe, knowing nothing about the battle between Buddhists and Moslems, eagerly accepted the tale of John the priest, or presbyter, 'King of the Indies'. And so one can imagine the sensation the arrival of a letter from this selfsame monarch caused in ecclesiastical and diplomatic circles. The letter arrived simultaneously at the court of the Emperor of Rome and of Byzantium from 'Prester John, by the grace of God most powerful king over all Christian kings'. The letter continued as follows:

Let it be known to you that we have the highest crown on earth as well as gold, silver, precious stones, and strong fortresses, cities, towns, castles, and boroughs. We have under our sway forty-two kings who are all mighty and good Christians. . . .

Our land is divided into four parts, for there are so many Indias. In Greater India lies the body of the Apostle Saint Thomas. . . . And this India is toward the east, for it is near the deserted Babylon and also near the tower called Babel.

Written in our holy palace in the land of Prester John.

One can imagine the effect of this royal epistle in the two world capitals of Rome and Byzantium. The news that Prester John actually existed and had offered his enormous resources in the cause of the holy war against the infidel was immediately transmitted to the courts of all Christian kings. The priest-king had suddenly become one of the most important personages in medieval Europe. Pope Alexander III hastened to reply to John's letter, calling him 'the illustrious and magnificent king of the Indies and a beloved son in Christ'. Other princes may also have sent their greetings to their new royal friend and envoys may have set forth to meet him. Geographers were now able to sketch in the 'Empire of Prester John' on their maps, and historians launched on elaborate biographies of the king descended from the Magi. And most important of all, since the Presbyter's dominions lay in the East – 'India' being a generic term for the unknown lands beyond the Tigris – it followed that this Christian monarch would be able to attack the Moslems from the rear, as, in fact, he had announced he intended to do.

It is not unreasonable, then, to suggest that Prester John's letter altered the whole balance of power in favour of the Christian nations and inspired new enthusiasm for the Crusade, and just as the commanders of the Christian armies were delighted with the military significance of an ally in the East, so the church historians were overjoyed to have the legend of St Thomas's mission to India confirmed by what appeared to be indisputable facts. For just as Peter was supposed to have taken Rome and Italy as his bailiwick, Mark Egypt, and James Spain, so Thomas had always been assigned India, which, some commentators had felt was overdoing the apostles' missionary work somewhat. Now the news that the whole of India and apparently the lands beyond were Christian was proof of St Thomas's martyrdom and corroboration of the other disciples' long journeys 'to the ends of the earth'.

And there was still another prize to be sought from the new eastern alliance – the prize of trade and commerce which no doubt to some was as important as the proof of St Thomas's mission to India. At all events explorers now set out to find the country of Prester John, the search lasting for some 500 years before it was finally abandoned. Among the first to take the road was the Venetian Marco Polo who followed the silk caravan route to Peking between 1271 and 1295, always hoping to get news of King John. Many others journeyed eastwards from Constantinople on the same mission throughout the 13th and 14th centuries until Henry the Navigator directed his sea captains to find an alternative route to India, round Africa. And even though none of these explorers ever reached the fabled land, the fame of Prester John in no way diminished, but increased as it became identified with, or merged into, the exploits of various Tartar or Mongol princes, like the Tartar warlord Yeh-lü Ta-Shih and the Mongol Ghengis Khan who, despite their crimes, were regarded throughout the Middle Ages as good Christian monarchs.

We know now that the attempts to find the kingdom of Prester John and the speculations as to who he was originated from that single bogus letter which arrived at the court of the Byzantine Emperor Manuel I (1143–80) and the Roman Emperor Frederick I (1152–90). The letter was in Latin, interspersed with some curious Graecisms, and it was quickly translated into all the principal European languages as well as into Hebrew.

Reading the letter today, one is astonished that it
was ever taken seriously by educated men, for to us it
is an obvious literary fiction, not unlike the Arabian
stories in *The Thousand Nights and a Night* or the
narratives of St George and the Dragon and other early
Christian miracle tales. But it is, of course, pointless
to read a 12th-century document in the light of modern
scholarship, since the whole attitude of mind in the
Middle Ages was different from, and, indeed, alien to,
our approach to history and religion. No doubt the
savants at the court of the Byzantine and Roman emperors were puzzled by the description of 'wild hares as
big as sheep; horses with two little horns; horned men
with an eye in the front and three or four in the back
of their heads; women who look similar; and people
who gobble up their father or mother without
troubling to cook either. . . .' But they were obviously
bedazzled by the many references to John's wealth,
his forty-two vassal kings, the extent of his dominions,
and his avowed intention to fight the enemies of
Christendom. Having been well and truly taken in by
this bombastic prelude, the clerics were in the right
frame of mind to accept with awe rather than scepticism Prester John's description of the 'Four Indias'
with their wild animals, monsters, and abominable
peoples of Gog and Magog; the pepper forests infested
with snakes; the herbs with which a man could con-
jure up the devil; the stone which made him invisible;
the ten lost tribes of Israel who were now subjects of
Prester John; the salamanders that spun threads for
the royal garments; and so forth.

As for the customs of this wondrous country, there were no thieves, robbers, or adulterers (obviously a numerous class in medieval society). The king had many beautiful wives, but he only slept with them – or some of them – four nights a year. His court consisted of 30,000 persons, the whole lot of whom sat down once a day to have a meal. The table at which they dined was made of emerald and rested on two columns of amethyst. It had the virtue of preventing drunkenness notwithstanding the quantity of wine consumed. At Prester John's right side sat twelve archbishops, at his left twenty-three bishops, including the Patriarch of St Thomas, the Bishop of Samarkand, and the Archbishop of Susa. Scattered about here and there were usually seven or more kings, scores of dukes, and hundreds of counts.

Interspersed with the description of Prester John's kingdom are a number of curious remarks which seem to have been popped in, as it were, either to annoy the Byzantines or as a kind of private joke. Thus the letter-writer uses the derogatory expression *Graeculi*, or 'petty Greeks' in referring to the subjects of the emperor Manuel I. The insult must have been intended by someone who was certainly well aware of the feuding between the Byzantines and Romans. The writer also asks, ironically, if King Manuel considers himself divine; and if so, how can he then possibly be a true Christian? Elsewhere – surely in a mock-serious vein? – he states that Prester John's butler was an archbishop as well as a king and his cook both a king and a prior. On the other hand, the elevated rank of these two menials is possibly referred to as the explanation of why this mighty emperor who ruled over forty-two vassal kings and 'as many lands as there were stars in the sky' desired to be addressed by the title of an elder of the church during the apostolic age. Hence Prester John should be read as Presbyter John, or John the Priest.

But while the descriptions of fabulous monsters seem absurd to us and the references to butlers who are archbishops and cooks who are kings almost ridiculous, they were nothing of the kind to people to whom the Orient was still a world of tremendous mystery. In other words, the medieval scholars withheld their judgment even on such matters as griffins and unicorns, both of which, says Prester John, abounded in his country. Since no one had visited these realms, they argued, how can we categorically deny that such beasts exist? Yes, we agree that the reference to 'bowmen who are men from the waist up and a horse from the waist down' sounds like a description of the Greek centaurs and it is admittedly hard to believe; but Prester John is an oriental monarch and orientals are notorious for exaggerations. . . .

So the scholars might have argued when called in by the Greek and Roman emperors to give their opinion as to the genuineness of the letter; and their verdict was that, in substance, it was undoubtedly genuine. From now on Prester John and his wondrous kingdom where lived horned men with three or four eyes in the back of their head was the Mecca of all adventurers. In particular, the commanders of the crusading armies in the Middle East were especially anxious to get in touch with their new ally. They never did, of course, and it was assumed by 1220 that Prester John himself must have died, leaving his throne to his son. In fact, news now came through in the intelligence reports of the army commanders that John's successor was called David and that this new king had successfully fought the Moslems on the far eastern frontiers capturing many cities, including Samarkand. King David was said to be marching on Baghdad, the capital of Islam. Thus do rumours flourish in wartime, and the farther they go, the stranger they become, so that just as the original rumour of the existence of Prester John seems to have begun with the victory of a Chinaman over an Arab, so the presence of King David, his son, no doubt derived from the attacks on Moslem cities like Samarkand by none other than Genghis Khan.

After looking for Prester John's domains for almost two centuries, it was agreed by the savants that the 'king of kings' was not to be found in Asia at all. Their conclusion, indeed, was now unavoidable, since none of the explorers from the time of Marco Polo had seen or heard even a hint of the fabulous monarch; and, as conclusive evidence, the Pope's personal investigator, the Dominican friar Jordanus de Severac, had made a special trip to India in 1325 without finding a trace of Prester John. But suddenly the mythical champion was born again, this time several thousand miles away in Africa: to be precise, in Ethiopia where he was to flourish for at least three centuries more. How he got from India to Ethiopia is not clear, unless it was that the friar Jordanus upon finding that there was no Prester John in the former country suggested that the Negus of Abyssinia must have been the person to whom Pope Alexander III had addressed his letter in 1177. The new location for the legendary king was, naturally, joyfully accepted by the Abyssinian monks at Jerusalem, though the more cautious Portuguese withheld their judgment until they had time to explore the entire African coast. As a precaution, however, Vasco da Gama on his voyage down the west coast of Africa in 1497 carried letters with him from King Emanuel I to His Royal Highness Prester John, though the great navigator never delivered these epistles.

And so by the beginning of the 16th century Asia had lost out as the land of this great Christian hero, who was supposed to help the Crusaders to annihilate the infidels for the greater glory of God. Asia by this time was fairly familiar to the missionaries, travellers, merchants, and geographers, and nobody of any intelligence believed any longer in the great and powerful kingdom of 'the Four Indias'. Ethiopia, on the other hand, was a perfect substitute and the legend of Prester John fitted that country like a glove. Ethiopia was unexplored, partially christianized, and in a position to threaten Moslem Egypt from the rear as the Indian Prester John had threatened Moslem Syria.

How, then, did this monarch get from India to Ethiopia without disillusioning all his admirers throughout Christian Europe? The answer is simple. Asia and Africa were not really separate continents at all to medieval geographers, but were divided by the Nile, so that Ethiopia was considered as part of 'India' where that country's name merely implied the 'East'. Hence a map of 1507 (the oldest in which the newly discovered continent of America is mentioned) places Prester John's empire somewhere in Tibet, with the words: 'This is the land of the good king and lord known as Prester John, lord of all eastern and southern India, in whose mountains are found all kinds of precious stones.' Exactly nine years later another map locates his country in Africa, and it was, of course, this location which kept the legend alive until the end of the 17th century. Thus Shakespeare undoubtedly believed that somewhere in the heart of Abyssinia lived a great Christian king called Prester John. In fact, the only Christians who did not believe that this was so were the Ethiopians themselves, for their ambassador who arrived in Rome in 1441 objected strenuously when his sovereign was referred to as 'John'. 'His true and only name is Zareiacob, meaning "Descendant of the prophet Jacob",' said the envoy, who knew nothing about a presbyter called John.

But this did not prevent either learned men or the common people from clinging to the legend that Prester John was reigning somewhere in the remote and mysterious Ethiopia, to which the Jesuit missionaries now began to make their way. But these priests, like those who had reached India, could find no trace of such a king, and as their reports gradually filtered

down to the public through the works of historians and
geographers, the legend slowly died away.

Even so, the subject is not closed; the inquiry still
goes on. To begin with, there are old colonies of Indian
Christians along the Malabar Coast, and these converts
have a legend of St Thomas's visit to their country
where he built a palace for a certain King Gundafor.
The king was converted to Christianity and his son
became a priest and thus was both priest and king on
his ascendancy to the throne. The Nestorian and
Syrian Christians, most of whose ancient records were
destroyed in the capture of Edessa by the Sultan Sanjar
in 1145, may have had in their archives some pertinent
facts concerning this Indian king, and we can at least
speculate as to whether this legend was not the origin
of the Prester John myth. In other words, if there was
an Indian king who had been converted to Christianity before the 10th century, news of this fact would
have been carried in the usual indefinite and exaggerated form by sailors across the Arabian Sea to the
Red Sea ports, from whence it would travel northwards
with the caravans to Antioch and Edessa. Then, in the
course of time, there would be added to these confused
reports the innumerable fictions taken from the hagi-
ology of the Eastern Church and the fairy tales told in
the bazaars. And finally, the legend reached Europe as
the myth of Prester John, the mighty emperor with a
vast army and inexhaustible wealth which he was
bringing to the aid of the Crusaders fighting to save not
only the sacred shrines, but Christendom itself.

So we see once again, and perhaps more clearly than

in the other cases of lost lands, how legends have a character of their own: how they seem to start from a seed of truth and grow like weeds into huge and sometimes fantastic proportions. As long as they are passed along by word of mouth – from a village in India to an Arab dhow at Mangalore, from there to an Arabian seaport and so always on by word of mouth to someone else – they are bound to be subject to changes and additions by each successive narrator. When the historian encounters them in written form, they are so encrusted not only with the growths of credulity and superstition but also with the various theories of the researchers that it is nearly always difficult to see where and why the legend started. This is especially true of the legend of Prester John whose name can still set us to wondering where he had his kingdom.

# Part Three

## *Lost Lands of the British Isles*

### 9: THE QUEST FOR THE CASSITERIDES

WE have seen that the ancient world was, to our way of thinking, particularly credulous when it came to myths and legends; and the reason was the absence of factual records on the one hand, and reliable observations of physical phenomena on the other. Not surprisingly, therefore, the various rumours concerning lost lands in the Atlantic and elsewhere were always of particular interest to the Greek and Roman geographers who were eager for every scrap of information they could get on the unexplored regions of the world. For in addition to the disadvantages of having to rely on travellers' tales, the cartographers faced tremendous technical problems in their efforts to work out some satisfactory format for their atlases. The principal difficulty confronting them, of course, was the lack of a reliable chronometer, or a timepiece of sufficient accuracy to make earth-measurements meaningful. Thus, long sea voyages can only be calculated by rough guesswork if the navigator has neither an accurate log, compass, nor clock. The ancient mariners had none of these instruments, and the wonder is that they had even a rough idea of the contours of the European coasts. Even so, they were at all times exceedingly curious about the lands to the north of the Mediterranean, since it was from these regions that the tin on which the early empires of the eastern Mediterranean depended for their weapons and tools of bronze.

Another difficulty for the geographers of the classical period resulted from the generally accepted belief that the Inhabited World, as the Greeks called it, was a roughly elliptical land mass surrounded by a circum-ambient river called the 'Ocean'. Even the greatest of the geographers accepted, in general, this concept of a disc-shaped earth whose land-mass ended in the west at the Pillars of Hercules and in the east with 'India beyond the Ganges'. Beyond lay the 'Ocean'.

It is easy to see why such a concept of the earth, floating like a log in a pond, according to Thales of Miletus, did not encourage exploration, just as the belief, held right up to the 15th century AD that the Atlantic reached boiling point below latitude twenty-six degrees, scarcely encouraged European navigators to voyage down the west coast of Africa. Yet new discoveries were made throughout the classical period, not as a result of scientific enterprise, but of military and commercial exploration. And one of these very early discoveries was due to the reports that there were rich deposits of tin in some mysterious islands which were said to be situated in the Atlantic Ocean.

The rumours of these islands must have been circulating in the ports of the Mediterranean from at least as early as 1,500 BC when ingots of tin arrived at the Greek port of Massilia (Marseilles) for trans-shipment to the manufactories in Crete, Assyria, and Egypt. The precious metal must have originally been carried overland across France, but when the Phoenicians got a hint as to its provenance, they set off in their ships to to find the actual place where it was mined. That they succeeded in their mission is suggested by a passage in Herodotus where he speaks of certain Tin Islands – the Cassiterides, as he calls them – though he admits that he has no knowledge of their whereabouts and even doubts whether they exist at all. But from that time on, the Cassiterides appear and re-appear in classical geographies, always with vague, and sometimes wildly inaccurate details of their position. Modern geographers have been trying to locate them ever since, for they are closely tied up with British history.

What were the Cassiterides and where were they? And are they the same as the lost islands of Celtic mythology?

It so happens that Greek and Roman geographers have left us with a number of clues sufficiently concrete to make the search both exciting and rewarding. For instance, a Sicilian writer named Diodorus who compiled a World History between 60 and 30 BC places the Cassiterides in the Ocean 'somewhere off the coast of Iberia (Spain) and north of Lusitania (Portugal)'. The Greek geographer Strabo, on the other hand, writing fifty or so years later, is more specific. He states that the Tin Islands were ten in number and that they lay close together in the open sea 'north of the harbour of the Artabri (probably Corunna)'. One of these islands was uninhabited; the others were occupied by people who wore black robes reaching down to their feet, were bearded like goats, and 'walked about with staves in their hands and the countenances of Furies in the tragedies' – which sounds like a specific reference to the British druids. Strabo adds that the people of the Cassiterides traded in tin and lead, receiving in exchange pottery, salt, and bronze vessels. The Phoenicians and Carthaginians, he says, were the main carriers of this trade until the Romans broke their monopoly after the expeditions of Caesar in 55 and 54 BC.

Did Strabo, then, place the Cassiterides in Britain?

Not exactly, since this writer's travels were limited to the coastal states of the Mediterranean, and he knew nothing about Britain except what he had read in Caesar's despatches. Moreover, Caesar himself did not know a great deal since he never conquered Britain. His deepest penetration made on the occasion of his second invasion with five legions and 2,000 cavalry was only as far inland as the Thames, somewhere about Kingston, where he succeeded in fording the river and capturing the headquarters of Cassivellaunus, the British tribal chieftain. Before the summer of 54 BC was ended, Caesar withdrew from Britain and the Roman armies did not land here again until the reign of Claudius about one hundred years later. Britain, in consequence, remained an unknown country, still quasi-mythical to the historians and geographers of the academies. The name itself was evocative of the mysterious and the marvellous, rather as Timbuctoo was to the 18th- and 19th-century geographers of Africa. Virgil in the *Eclogues* refers to the Britons as being almost wholly cut off from the rest of the world, and Latin writers right up to the disintegration of the old empire invariably refer to our country as a fog-enshrouded island at the end of the inhabited world. In fact, an ordinary Greek or Roman of the 1st century AD would have regarded an ancient Briton much as the Victorians regarded a Fuzzy-Wuzzy of the Sudan.

But the clues are still forthcoming. Another historian, this time the Spaniard Pomponius Mela (AD 43–104), states that the Cassiterides were situated *in Celticis*, 'in the lands of the Celts', which is not very helpful, as ancient writers used the name *Celts* to include the Irish, British, and North European peoples west of the Rhine. Pliny the Elder (AD 23–79) who was, in any case, more of an encyclopaedist than a geographer, places the Cassiterides 'over against Celtiberia'. (That is, north central Spain.) Ptolemy (2nd century AD), on the other hand, copies Strabo and states that the Tin Islands, ten in number, are situated in the Western Ocean. It is astonishing that a scientist of Ptolemy's ability should be so vague about northern Europe almost 200 years after Julius Caesar had landed in Britain until it is remembered that none of the Greek or Roman geographers had ever travelled north of the Alps or had ever visited the British Islands. Hence they were obliged to rely on previous authors, in particular the only one who gave an eyewitness account of the Atlantic islands, the explorer Pytheas of the Greek colony of Massilia.

It was undoubtedly the rivalry of Massilia, first with Phoenician Tyre and later with the Punic colony of Carthage, that inspired the expedition of Pytheas in the 4th century BC, with orders to spy on the Phoenicians' Atlantic trade and, if possible, to discover their sources of tin and amber. Pytheas reached Britain, presumably circumnavigated it, then sailed on six days northwards to an island called Thule beyond which the sea turned into frozen slush. His account of Britain and lands still farther to the north was as significant to both the scientific and mercantile class of the pagan world as Columbus's voyage to the Americas was to Renaissance Europe. The nature of his discovery, in fact, was almost precisely the same: it was the result of crossing a frontier hitherto regarded as impassable.

It is no wonder, therefore, that the geographers whose concept of the world was still based on the Aristotelian thesis that the sea beyond the Pillars of Hercules was unnavigable rejected the extraordinary and, to them, fantastic, account of Pytheas as a tissue of fables, if not of lies. Pytheas, in fact, seems to have aroused the outright hostility of the leading authorities of both his own and subsequent periods, which may explain why all copies of the original of his exploration called *On the Ocean* have disappeared. Now, to our regret, we only learn of it through the prejudiced notices of the explorer's critics – notably Polybius, Strabo, and Pliny. In other words, Pytheas was dismissed by savants for the next 500 years as a sort of

Baron Munchausen, whence it is not surprising that his narrative was less and less read until it was ignored altogether and disappeared from the great libraries of the ancient world.

Yet enough remains of the work, even if second hand, to show that Pytheas of Marseilles did discover the British Islands – and one makes this statement despite the probability that the Phoenicians had already reached the Cornish coasts long before the Greek explorer set out from Massilia around 340 BC. But the Phoenician sailors knew no more about Britain than Columbus's crew knew about the United States: they only knew this far northern land as a small tin-producing island which they reached by sailing up the coast of Spain north from Tartessus. They must have crossed the English Channel probably from the Cherbourg Peninsula and, having made a landfall off Cornwall, they anchored where they could load the ingots of tin aboard their galleys. This seems to have been the extent of their knowledge of Britain.

Pytheas, on the other hand, gives precise information about his voyage from the time he left his home-port, information apparently recorded, in modern fashion, as a ship's log. He tells us, for instance, that the distance from Marseilles to the Straits of Gibraltar is 7,000 *stadia* if sailed in a direct line. The precise length of a Greek *stadium* has not yet been determined, but it is usually accepted as 194 English yards. Roughly, therefore, one nautical mile equals ten *stadia*. The actual distance between Marseilles and Gibraltar is 800 miles, so Pytheas's calculations were some 100

miles out. Considering the absence of anything resembling modern navigational aids, this is not such a
bad error.

Having passed through the Straits, Pytheas sailed
northwards along the coast as far up as the Sacred Promontory (Cape St Vincent), rightly considered by the
ancients to be the westernmost point of continental
Europe and hence of the inhabited world. As soon as
Pytheas had crossed the Bay of Biscay, however, he
reported that another headland projected out still farther into the Atlantic, a cape he called Calbion which
he conjectured was 2,000 *stadia* (200 miles) west of the
Sacred Promontory. He was badly out in his geography
here, since Ushant (Ouessant) is actually 230 miles *east*
of Cape St Vincent. What may have happened is that
he had been swept eastwards by the tides thinking that
he was sailing in a straight line due north.

One should never, however, make categorical statements about the geography of the ancients, since, as
we have pointed out, their navigators and scientists
were confronted with insurmountable difficulties in
fixing precise positions by latitude and longitude, let
alone in estimating such geophysical features as distance and contours of coasts, hills, and mountain
ranges. Hence, all their positions are really the out-
come of inspired guesses. Yet Pytheas did fix the latitude of his home-town Marseilles within a few seconds,
using the simple surveyor's rod, or gnomon, as a sun-
dial. He also calculated the relationship between the
moon and the tides in the Atlantic; determined as best
he could the configuration of the British Islands; and

reported many ethnographical and geographical facts concerning the unknown countries of northern Europe, so that the account of his voyage is, as we shall see, an important clue as to the whereabouts of the islands called the Cassiterides.

He tells us, for instance, that he crossed from the Continent to Britain in twenty-four hours. This is just about the time it takes a sailing vessel today to run with a fair wind from Ushant in Brittany to Mount's Bay in Cornwall, the distance being around 120 sea miles, the course north by west, the speed around five knots.

Pytheas also gave particulars concerning the Cornish peninsula, to which he gave the name Belerion, a name which it retained throughout the classical age. In addition, he established the roughly triangular configuration of the main island, which suggests that he did actually circumnavigate it in a clockwise direction before sailing on eastwards to the mouth of the River Elbe in search of the countries from whence came the amber so highly prized not only as an ornament but as a cure for many diseases. Again, in the best tradition of Greek science, he observed and measured as many phenomena as he could, giving the shape and measurements of Britain as in Figure 2, on the next page.

If these figures which have come down to us are correct, Pytheas was out in all his measurements, as one would expect where distances are based on dead reckoning – that is on the estimated day's sail. His aids, too, for surveying were primitive: he could only work with the gnomon and clepsydra. So it is not surprising

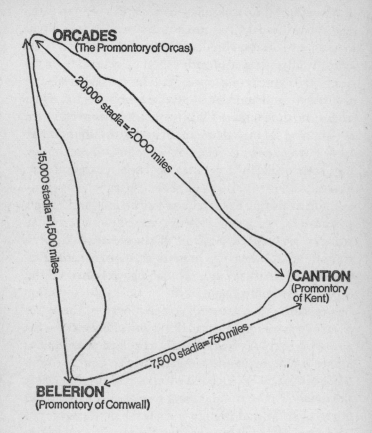

FIGURE 2

**BRITAIN ACCORDING TO PYTHEAS**

that his report that the tide around the British coasts rose to the prodigious height of 80 cubits, or 120 feet, made him the object of scorn to the academicals back in the ports of the Mediterranean where there was scarcely any tide at all. But Pytheas may actually have seen a particularly high spring tide in the Bristol Channel where the rise and fall has been recorded at sixty feet; so that the explorer was correct if he was referring to the rise plus the fall of water round certain parts of the western coast.

His observations concerning Britain, then, were valuable and reasonably accurate. He noted the greyness of the skies, even in summer; the fact that the rains at harvest necessitated the threshing of grain in barns instead of outdoors; the production of beer from fermented grain; the paucity of domestic animals in the far north of the island; and the reliance of the northern Britons on oats.

But perhaps his most important discovery from the point of view of the merchants back in Marseilles was the secret of the Phoenicians' tin trade and the precise route of that commerce from the Cornish mines to the Mediterranean markets. His report also proves conclusively that the tin trade was in full operation in the 4th century BC and had, in fact, been conducted for so long that the Britons engaged in it were relatively civilized and friendly to foreign visitors. There could be no stronger evidence that the Cassiterides were somewhere in the western part of Britain and that both the Phoenicians and their colonists the Carthaginians continued to trade with the Cornish tin mines until

the Romans closed the Straits of Gibraltar to their
ships.

So did the Phoenicians know the whereabouts of the
Cassiterides?

The Roman geographer Avienus, writing in the 4th
century of our era, states that 'nobody has sailed his
ship into the Atlantic Ocean, the greatest of seas, because it is inhabited by a crowd of monsters who terrify
the very coasts'.

But the Phoenicians, the most daring and skilful
sailors of antiquity, paid scant attention to these old
wives' tales. The location of their colonies all across
the Mediterranean shows that they had the ships and
men capable of making long sea voyages. Their merchantmen, for instance, were equipped with sails and
200 oars. They had, too, their own secrets of navigation,
for they had made a scientific study of ocean travel
comparable with that undertaken by Henry the Navigator in the mid-15th century: in short, they documented all the information concerning tides, currents,
landmarks, reefs and so forth as the data were brought
in by their captains. They also put to practical use the
observations of the Assyrian and Egyptian astronomers.
Hence the Phoenicians were able to steer by the comparatively feeble star Polaris within the Little Bear
constellation, whereas the Greeks continued to use the
brighter stars of the Great Bear. Their galleys were
thus able to put well out to sea, using the sun by day
as a navigational aid and the North Star at night, to
give them more precise bearings.

And if proof were required of either the seaworthiness of the Punic ships or the skill of their navigators, we have records of voyages far longer than the run up the Atlantic coast of Europe from Tartessus to Cornwall. In 600 BC, during the reign of the pharoah Neccho, they seem to have circumnavigated Africa, leaving by the Red Sea and returning through the Straits of Gibraltar, taking three years on this voyage of exploration. Around 450 BC, the admiral Hanno cruised down the west coast of Africa perhaps as far as the Congo, from which they brought back the skin of a gorilla to be hung in the temple of Moloch in Carthage. Both of these tremendous voyages were undertaken for purposes of trade.

So if the Phoenicians did come to Britain, it was because they knew this island was the richest source of tin in Europe, and tin to the empires of the Bronze Age was what oil is to empires today. But it is certain that these old sea traders kept their supply sources and the routes thither a closely guarded trade secret. In fact, the Romans repeatedly tried to discover the Phoenician route to the Cassiterides without success, until Publius Licinius Crassus, one of Caesar's lieutenants in Gaul, sailed across to Britain on orders to reconnoitre the island in preparation for Caesar's invasion. But by this time, the Phoenician and Carthaginian fleets had been swept from the seas, and, for that matter, Cornish tin was no longer in great demand. Times had changed. Weapons were now being made from iron, not bronze; and tin was being mined in sufficient quantities in north-west Spain, Portugal, and Brittany.

From the time of the Roman occupation of Britain, the Cassiterides disappeared from the map.

None the less, modern historians, with the aid of the archaeologists, have searched long and carefully to find these lost islands on the basis of the undisputed fact that the Phoenicians obtained their tin there. A French prehistorian and authority on Punic matters, conducted numerous excavations in the Scilly Islands and Cornwall and found nothing. His lack of success was not surprising. The Phoenicians, unlike the Romans, were not interested in conquering or colonizing the countries with which they traded, so it is no use looking for imposing monuments left by their merchants in Britain, any more than it is in southern Spain where they had their most important outposts at Cadiz, Cartegna, and Tartessus.

Some excitement was engendered, however, when a bronze bull was dug up in the vicar's garden at St Just in Penwith, Cornwall, in 1832. This little bull, though only two inches high, was acclaimed as a Phoenician artefact; and it is arguable that this effigy did come with the Phoenicians as one of the gee-gaws which their traders bartered to primitive people in exchange for native products. In any case, it would be interesting to know how a bronze bull of this provenance and antiquity finished up in a vicarage garden in a village not far from Land's End.

More suggestive of a direct link between Africa and Cornwall is the bronze coin supposed to have been unearthed at Cara Brea, the great prehistoric hill castle also near Land's End. This coin (like the bronze bull, now in the Truro Museum) has a bearded head on one side and a galloping horse on the reverse, and is usually atributed to the Numidian king Micipsa who reigned over a Phoenician colony from 248–228 BC. The head is of the king and the horse is presumably symbolic of the famous African cavalry which fought first for Carthage and then for Rome. It is conceivable that this coin reached Cornwall in the purse of a Punic merchant who did not, of course, use it for trading with the Britons, but who simply dropped it by accident. Not surprisingly, the antiquarians call this Numidian piece 'puzzling'.

But we do have one important and specific clue to the whereabouts of the Cassiterides in a statement of the Sicilian historian Diodorus who gives this description of the British tin trade:

Now we shall speak about the tin that is mined there.

The inhabitants of the promontory called Belerion [i.e. Cornwall], by reason of their converse with merchants, are more civilized and courteous to strangers than the rest of the Britons.

These are the people that produce the tin which with a great deal of care and labour they dig out of the ground. The ground, incidentally, is quite rocky, and the metal has to be melted down, and refined, after which it is beaten into ingots shaped like an *astragalus*, and carried to a near-by island called Ictis. For at low water this island and the mainland are connected, enabling carts loaded with tin to pass over. . . . The exporters load the tin into vessels at Ictis and transport the cargo to France where it goes overland on pack horses to the mouth of the River Rhone.

The important name here is obviously Ictis, which some commentators have supposed is a false reading for *Vectis*, the Roman name of the Isle of Wight. But the Wight was certainly never joined to the mainland at low water within recorded time, so carts could not have crossed over by land. Moreover, there would have been no point in carrying the tin 200 miles or more from the Cornish mines to the Isle of Wight for trans-shipment to the Continent when there were good harbours in the locality of the mines themselves. So geographers have accepted the form *Ictis* and identified it with St Michael's Mount in Mount's Bay. Their identification of the 'island called Ictis' with the Cassiterides is supported by the evidence that the carting of tin from the near-by mines on the mainland across to St Michael's Mount for loading aboard ships was still going on in the last decades of the 19th century. As for the ingots of tin shaped like an *astragalus*, it so happens that a large lump of tin weighing 158 pounds was dredged up from Falmouth Bay in 1812. The ingot is slightly concave in shape, like a saddle, and was probably cast in this manner to make it easier to load on the back of the donkeys which carried the tin from the mines to the port of St Michael's Mount.

Was this Cornish haven, then, the place where the Phoenician galleys anchored? And were the headlands of Belerion, wich appeared to be islands when seen from the sea, the origin of the myth of the lost Cassiterides?

## 10: ST BRENDAN'S ISLAND

O N many of the charts published in the 17th and early 18th centuries, an island called St Brendan's was marked as lying somewhere near 'Antilia' in the western Atlantic. In fact, Columbus himself refers to this island in his diary, with the implication that he expected to sight it on his voyage to the Americas. Even stranger, the Portuguese Crown actually laid claim to sovereignty over this territory, though they admitted that its exact location remained to be discovered, for which reason they despatched four expeditions between 1526 and 1721 to find it. Indeed, they were so certain of its existence that they had already sold off lots on St Brendan's Island to sundry noble families whose names were duly registered in the state archives. So far the island has never been found, and the descendants of the original purchasers of land there are still presumably waiting for their allotment.

How, then, did this curious mistake arise? How did St Brendan's Island get on to the official charts? And who was Brendan?

The answer to these questions takes us back almost fourteen centuries to an obscure hamlet in western Ireland and to a period which the older historians designate the Dark Ages. For such is the place and time that we first hear of an obscure Irish monk after whom an island was once named.

But not so obscure at that! For considering the circumstances, we know a good deal about this priest who, if the legend is true, made one of the great voyages of history. We know that Brendan was born around the middle of the 5th century and became attached to a monastery near Tralee on the west coast of Ireland at an early age. We even know the name of his tutors, all of them recorded in the Irish church annals: their names, St Ita, Bishop Erc, and St Jarlach of Tuam.

And so the young Brendan grew up and was educated during the 'Age of the Saints' in Ireland, an age of great intellectual activity when the rest of Europe was in collapse at the end of the Roman Empire. Obviously Roman learning – its science and art – had still not been lost or suppressed at this time, particularly in Ireland which was far from the scenes of war and destruction attendant on the decline and eventual fall of the world's greatest empire. We may be sure that Brendan's tutors, like all the early Christian divines, were well versed in the orthodox theology and, by the same token, were scornful of pagan literature with its questionable gods and even more questionable morality. But it seems that they had heard of the Greco-Roman Isles of the Blest, which they transformed into the idea of a Christian commonwealth, a utopia which Brendan was to spend his life searching for. The records of his famous voyages tell us that he finally succeeded; and the proof that he did – in the eyes of the 18th-century map-makers, at least – was the inclusion on the charts of St Brendan's Island in the western Atlantic. So appears, and disappears, in history one of the strangest of the lost islands of antiquity.

Yet irrespective of the geographical evidence that

denies all knowledge of the saintly explorer's island, whether above or below the Atlantic waves, the legend which sprang up around his name and, even more, the account of his voyages which have come down to us continue to fascinate the searchers after the hard core of the truth which is hidden behind the incrustation of the myth. In the first place, the legend does have overtones of similar folk-tales from classical days, including Plato's account of a lost island-kingdom, which is no longer dismissed as pure fantasy. In the second place, the Brendan saga surely belongs in that area of exploration, some of it speculative, some documented, which includes the expeditions of the Norsemen and Celts who undoubtedly made some of the greatest voyages and most important discoveries in history. Admittedly, partly because of the lack of precise records and partly because of the exaggerations of legend, the actual achievements of the Norsemen and of Irish monks like St Brendan have never been, and probably never can be, properly assessed; so that while it is conceivable that St Brendan reached Iceland according to some commentators and America according to others, it is conversely arguable that the account of his whole voyage was pure fiction. In the face of so many unknowns, we can only examine the evidence and keep an open mind, glancing back, perhaps, at the controversy that still surrounds the problem of Atlantis.

The facts given us in the biography of the saint are that after his ordination he set out with fourteen other monks on his first voyage to what is called the *terra repromissionis sanctorum*, the promised land of the saints, but he does not seem to have succeeded. Instead, he returned to his convent and continued his life as an ascetic and teacher, until, at the age of eighty-one, after he had founded his own monastery at Clonfert, he heard the call again and set off, a second time, in company with thirty-three chosen companions in skin-covered coracles. This floating monastery was gone for over eight years before Brendan reached his longed-for destination.

What islands he touched at in his long voyage and where he finally finished his odyssey remains a matter of controversy. Some students of the text of his *Navigatio* (as the account of his expedition is called) argue that he reached the Canary Islands, or the classical Isles of the Blest. Others again interpret the descriptions of the places he describes as referring to Iceland, Greenland, and even the North American continent. But all agree that Brendan – with a few companions, since thirty-three seems rather a large number to float about in coracles – did sail from the west coast of Ireland.

To undertake a long journey in a coracle seems to us inconceivable, but it is an historical fact that there was a regular traffic in these craft between Ireland and Britain. This fact is attested to by an entry in the *Anglo-Saxon Chronicle* for the year 891 stating that three 'Scots' came from Ireland in a coracle 'bent on serving God by means of a pilgrimage'. King Alfred interviewed them, and we even know the names of these intrepid pilgrims who paddled across the St

George's and Bristol Channels to land in Cornwall: they were Dubslane, Macbeth, and Maelinmum. We should not, then, think of St Brendan's voyage as impossible even though attempts to find his island, as we have seen, were not finally abandoned until 1759, after which date it no longer appears on the official maps.

What, then, do we know of a positive nature about St Brendan's voyage? It could be said by the more sceptical reader that the *Navigatio Brendani* reads like a tall story as told by an old sailor who had only the vaguest idea of where he had travelled. Neither latitude nor longitude are mentioned: direction and distance can only be guessed at. And yet, remembering that the *Navigatio* may have been first set down nearly ten centuries before any systematic exploration of the Atlantic Ocean was undertaken by Prince Henry the Navigator, how does one explain away as pure legend such descriptions of phenomena like this? 'The island they came upon three days later seemed quite near at hand but turned out to be a good three days' journey away. When they reached it, Brendan gazed upwards, but could hardly see the top because of its great height: it was higher than the sky and seemed to be made of pure crystal.'[32] Is this the description of an iceberg? Or of the ice-covered mountains of Greenland?

Elsewhere the narration refers to an island in eruption – 'when they looked from afar, they saw the mountain, clear of clouds, vomiting forth flames sky-high and then sucking them back upon itself, so that the whole mass of rock, right down to the sea level, glowed like a pyre.' This certainly sounds like the description of a phenomenon no Irishman who stayed at home could have witnessed.

In fact, on the strength of these references to icebergs and volcanoes, some commentators have not only accepted *in toto* the theory that St Brendan reached North America in his coracle by way of Iceland, but have set out to follow up the clues which they submit as evidence of the white man's presence in the New World long before Columbus discovered America and even before the Norsemen landed in Greenland. The so-called 'megalithic ruins' at North Salem near Boston, Massachusetts, are cited as proof that New England was the site of a monastery built by 'Irish monks', though a rival school of amateur archaeologists argues for the existence of a Phoenician temple. Unfortunately for the adherents of both theories, the ruins in question which cover about an acre and consist of dry stone chambers and walls are such as any competent farmer could build: the mystery, if there is one, is who troubled to construct this primitive complex of chambers and walls? And did he intend to hoax the experts? If so, he did not succeed, for it is now agreed that these ruins have nothing to do with Phoenician colonists or Irish monks. They were undoubtedly the work of an eccentric New England farmer in the last century.

So much, then, for the attempts to find some positive clues of St Brendan's voyages. Does the absence of them invalidate the *Navigatio* altogether? The mythologists think not. They contend that the manuscript should not be read as a ship's log, but as an amalgam of ancient Celtic legends telling of sea journeys made by

Irish missionaries across to Scotland, Wales, England, and Brittany, and possibly as far as Iceland and the Azores. True, it would seem at first glance that such long voyages in the open sea, in round boats made of skins and without a compass, would be unthinkable; but we must not judge the ability and intrepidity of the mariners of ancient times by seamanship as it is understood today. The Irish like the Vikings, grew up on the Atlantic coasts and the sea did not have the same terrors for them as it did, for instance, to the Egyptians in their day and even the Romans in theirs. Neither nation were blue water sailors, whereas the western Celts and the Scandinavians lived by and on the ocean.

And so we can assume, with whatever reservations we think fit, that St Brendan made a long voyage which so deeply impressed his countrymen that the memory of his exploits was never forgotten in the place from whence he set forth. We can assume, too, that by the 10th century when the monks of the abbey of Clonfert issued an official account of his *Navigatio*, his adventures had got wildly exaggerated and confused with the myths of the Fortunate Islands, the Isles of the Blest, Avalon, and other lost lands embedded in the folk-memory of the Celtic people. So the legend grew and was accepted as true throughout the Christian world. *The Voyage of St Brendan* was translated into all the principal foreign languages, English, Welsh, French, Spanish, German; and its influence continued to be exerted even on those practical-minded medieval navigators whose job was to chart the islands in the

Atlantic. And so, St Brendan's Island remained on the map, for the Irish saint's legend died hard for reasons that we shall see in the next chapter.

## II: AVALON AND THE ISLANDS OF THE DEAD

### *Avalon*

B E F O R E going on to examine the evidence for other lost worlds, it is worth our while to pause for a moment in order to note the difference between the legend of Plato and that of St Brendan: between the mentality of a great philosopher and that of an Irish saint. For it is this difference which helps us to understand why the search for Atlantis on the one hand seems worth while and the quest for St Brendan's Island on the other has long since been abandoned. The difference, then, is that the legends which have come to us from classical times are clear, concise, and comprehensible within the framework of history and geography. In contrast, those that have come down to us in the form of early Celtic folk-tales are so overlaid with incredible happenings and absurd details that we are inclined to dismiss the whole lot as pure fiction.

But if we are agreed that the 'myths' of Atlantis, the Garden of Eden, and the Fortunate Islands all have their origin in actual historical events and geographical locations, we should apply the same principle to Celtic folk-lore. In other words, St Brendan's voyage, irrespective of whether he reached Iceland or the Azores, does record an Irish monk's search for a new world which he probably intended to convert to Christianity. And so with the other Celtic versions of what we can generalize as the 'Atlantis myth'. For they all have one thing in common: they tell of an island which always lies to the west, an island rich in food and the beauties of nature, where no unpleasantness exists, and men are god-fearing and virtuous. In some legends of these mysterious and half-lost lands, it is living men, like St Brendan, who set out to find them; in others, they have become the abode of the dead.

Typical of these islands as described in Celtic myths was Avalon, the Elysian retreat to which King Arthur was borne away to be healed of his wounds. He was transported by boat after the Battle of Camlon and, significantly, the pilot on this voyage was the same Barinthus who piloted Brendan on his expedition. Avalon, then, was still another name for that mysterious island which lay to the west and which appears again and again in Celtic, as it does in classical, mythology. In the Old Irish legends this ideal land was also known as the 'Field of Happiness'. 'The Land of Youth', and so forth, and it invariably corresponds closely to all the Atlantis or Garden of Eden myths.

## Brittia

Even so, Avalon remains for us a never-never land, simply because, as we have mentioned above, Celtic myths have passed through so many phases – from prehistoric to early Christian – that their probable core of fact has been lost under a thick covering of improbable detail. We can understand, therefore, the bewilderment of those classical writers, Julius Caesar among them, who attempted to get to the bottom of Celtic history, customs, and folk-lore. One detects the puzzlement of a sophisticated Roman in Caesar's description, for instance, of the Druids who burnt their sacrificial victims in wicker-baskets. What kind of people would do this sort of thing in the name of religion?

In fact, we can see how perplexing the Celtic and German legends of unknown lands were to the Greeks and Romans in the few references we have to them in the classical writers. In this respect, we should remember that in the clear and sunny light of the Mediterranean world these mist-shrouded islands of northern Europe were more the abode of ghosts than of men, a notion which is very clearly conveyed in a curious passage in the *War of the Goths* by Procopius, the 6th-century Byzantine historian. Procopius tells of a country he calls Brittia, which he places between Britannia and the island of Thule. This is the country, he says, to which the Britons take their dead, and he certainly makes it sound like a first-rate ghost story.

All at once, during the night, they hear a knock on the door of their houses and a faint voice that calls them to their work. Immediately rising from their beds, they go down to the sea shore as though hypnotized by an unseen force. And here they see ships ready to sail but without a crew. Next they go aboard these foreign vessels and begin to row, noting that the ships seem to be loaded down with a multitude of unseen passengers, so that the water is practically up to the gunwales.

At no time do they see a single person, but after an hour's rowing they reach the island and the unseen passengers go ashore. The Britons say that they hear a voice announcing the name of all those who have made the crossing and describing the dignities which they held in life and calling them ashore by their hereditary titles. And also if a woman happens to cross over with them, they call over the names of their dead husbands who come forward to meet them.

Where, one wonders, is this 'Brittia' (spelt *Brettia* in some manuscripts)? It is impossible to locate from Procopius's statement, since his knowledge of the geography of northern Europe was almost nil. He even puts Britannia 'somewhere towards the setting sun, at the extremity of the country of the Spaniards, distant from the continent of Europe not less than 453 miles'. And then, where did he pick up this strange story which has all the hallmarks of a Christian version of the old Greek myth of the River Styx?

The best guess is that he was vaguely talking about Ireland which the 4th-century historian Avienus calls the 'Sacred Island'. Certainly Procopius's description of the dead being ferried across to some holy land is characteristic of Celtic mythology; and equally certain, Ireland, the only country of north-western Europe which the Romans apparently never visited, was always the mystery island of antiquity, since it lay over what was supposed to be the rim of the world. In fact, nothing positive was known about the British Isles at all until Julius Caesar made his reconnaissance in 55 BC, and sent back the first 'official' report to Rome. But the Roman general admits that he was unable to obtain any very useful information, either from the British or their Gaulish allies as to the size of the island, the character and strength of the tribes which inhabited it, their manner of fighting, their customs, and the harbours suitable for his invasion fleet. We can be sure that the natives had good reasons for withholding information from the Romans, one of which was certainly the existence of the highly profitable Irish gold mines; for, unbeknown to the Romans, the Irish had been mining and exporting gold to the Continent for a thousand years or more, the trade routes running from Ireland to North Cornwall, overland across Britain to the Straits of Dover, by ship to France, and from there to the courts of the kings and tribal chieftains throughout northern Europe. Naturally the British and Gallic merchants were not giving away the secret of this lucrative trade, and the Romans never really discovered it, otherwise they might have decided to invade and occupy Ireland. As it was, that country remained a mystery throughout the entire classical period, and it is typical of that time that one Roman historian describes it as the 'sacred land' and another asserts that its inhabitants were cannibals. Nearer the truth was the claim that Ierne was a country of rich pastures and warlike people, so warlike, says one commentator that mothers placed the first morsel of food into their newborn son's mouth on the tip of their husband's sword.

This, then, was the sort of vague information that the classical writers had managed to obtain about Ireland, which continued to be the source of many legends of lost lands, as it was a half-lost land itself even after the Romans had pacified and civilized Britain.


## Lyonnesse

Once the Romans had withdrawn their legions from Britain around the beginning of the 5th century AD, all attempts on the part of their historians and geographers to solve the mystery of undiscovered places like the Cassiterides, Thule, Brittia, and Ierne were abandoned. The scholars of Rome, Athens, and Alexandria now had other things on their mind as the enemies of the empire crossed the frontiers, while the commanders of the legions fought among themselves for the throne of the Caesars.

Britain now became even more isolated from the Mediterranean than it was before, particularly the western parts of the island where the old legends as recorded by writers like Diodorus, Avienus, and Procopius were replaced by, or merged into, new versions of lost lands. Possibly the folk-memory of the Cassiterides of the Phoenicians became in time the legend of Lyonnesse, a mythical country which is situated in almost precisely the same region. Lyonesse, in short, was the name of a submerged peninsula which once joined the Cornish mainland with the Scilly Isles – and it is interesting to note here that some commentators believe that the Scillies, and not St Michael's Mount, were the Cassiterides of the Phoenician tin trade.

As for the theory that the Scillies were joined to the mainland, the geological evidence shows that this was not unlikely, as the rocks of the Seven Stones reef mid-way between the two places indicate.

We first hear something definite about this sub-merged region from an early English chronicler called William of Worcester who seems to have wandered all over England in the 15th century collecting snippets of gossip and legend from manuscripts in the monastery libraries. As this was prior to the dissolution of these great centres of learning, William had access to sources which have since been destroyed or lost; and one of the sources he consulted was the library of the monastery on St Michael's Mount in Cornwall. In his book of memoranda called the *Itinerary*, he quotes extracts from a document he saw in the archives of St Michael's stating that 'there were formerly woods and fields and 140 parochial churches, all now submerged, between the Mount and the Isles of Scilly'.

Some critics maintain that the documents William saw were only copies of manuscripts housed in the library of the parent-abbey of Mont-Saint-Michel in Normandy where similar legends of great inundations along the French Atlantic coast had been recorded by the French monks. The best known of these quasi-mythical events refers to the disappearance beneath the sea of Ys, a splendid city said to have been situated in early Christian times on the shores of what is now the Bay of Trespasses. Was Lyonnesse, then, simply the English counterpart of the City of Ys, which the Cor-nish monks had confused with folk tales concerning the Cassiterides, Avalon, and Lyonesse? If so, the legend died hard, for 150 years after William of Worcester's report, we find the Cornish antiquary Richard Carew still convinced that a land bridge had once joined Land's End to the Scillies. He writes in his *Survey of Cornwall*:

Lastly, the encroaching sea hath ravined from it [i.e. from Cornwall] the whole country of Lioness, together with divers other parcels of no little circuit; and that such a Lioness there was, these proofs are yet remaining.

The space between the Land's End and the Isles of Scilly, being about 30 miles, to this day retaineth that name in Cornish – Lethowsow – and carrieth continually an equal depth of 40–60 fathoms, a thing not usual in the sea's proper dominion. Save that midway there lieth a rock, which at low water discovereth his head. . . . Fishermen casting their hooks thereabouts have drawn up pieces of doors and windows. Moreover the ancient name of Saint Michael's Mount was Cara Clowse in Cowse: in English The Hoare Rocke in the Wood: which is now at every flood encompassed by the sea, and yet at some low ebbs, rootes of mightie trees are descried in the sands about it.

Again, one is inclined to question the likelihood of Carew's fishermen bringing up 'pieces of doors and windows'; or, if they did, such flotsam would have been much more likely to have come from the frequent wrecks around this treacherous coast, not to mention the infamous practice of deliberately luring ships on to the rocks. But the reference to the unusual geology of the area – the depth of water and vestiges of trees in the sands – is not so easily disposed of. In fact, some fifty years ago the archaeologist O. G. S. Crawford made a special study of the Lyonnesse myth and came to the conclusion that 'there are good reasons for believing that the substance of the legend is true: that within prehistoric times there did actually exist land which is now covered by the sea'.[33] Mr Crawford went to the Scilly Isles himself in order to investigate some of the reports which have been in circulation for centuries among the natives of Cornwall and which are invariably dismissed as hearsay by outsiders. He found that these reports were usually more credible than Carew's 'pieces of doors and windows': that is, they were based on the sighting of boles of trees, walls, stone huts, and the like at the time of Low Water Springs when the ebb tide recedes farthest. Mr Crawford tells us that in 1926 he crossed from St Mary's, the largest of the Scillies, to the uninhabited island of Samson, from the highest point of which he observed, stretching across the uncovered sandflats between Sansom and Tresco, a long straight line of stones which, on closer examination, turned out to be a man-made wall. On the sands near by he picked up a number of flint flakes. Here was proof that these flats now submerged at half-tide were once dry land, for nobody would build a mile-long wall in the sea. The wall, Mr Crawford believes, served the same use that walls on dry land in this part of Britain do today, since it is built in exactly the same manner of the same materials. It was, in short, a stone 'hedge' for dividing up fields. Such 'hedges' are one of the most characteristic aspects of the British country-side from Land's End to John o' Groats, and they have been constructed from prehistoric times up to the recent past by placing large stone slabs upright some few yards apart and carefully filling in the space between with boulders and smaller stones. The job is not as simple as it looks and requires the skill of generations passed down from father to son.

Obviously, then, the boulder-hedge that Mr Crawford found on Samson flats could not have been built when the sands were periodically flooded by the tide. The explanation can only be that it was constructed when this region of the Scillies known as the 'inland sea' (i.e., the shallow basin between the main islands of Tresco, St Martins, and St Mary's) was a level plain covered with a thin layer of earth and above sea level. This plain was eroded by the south-west gales, the whole area subsided, and all vestiges of human habitation were covered by sand. However, under certain climactic conditions and at certain states of the spring tides, the appearance of tree stumps and the wall across the Samson flats in the Scillies, like the partially submerged stone circles at Er Lanis in Brittany, all prove the credibility of the Celtic folk-memories of lost cities and lands – of the Breton legend of Ys and the Cornish legend of Lyonnesse.

Lyonnesse, then, is a most interesting example of how legend is made, beginning with the faint memory of ancient days as passed down by word of mouth to succeeding generations; picked up and embellished by local antiquarians; accepted as authentic in an age addicted to myth and magic; and finally formalized by poets and story-tellers. The entire history of Lyonnesse can be traced in this manner from its geological begin-

nings with the subsidence of coastal regions all round
Cornwall and the Scilly Isles to Tennyson's epic poem
*Idylls of the King*. In between, the ancient inundation
legend had provided the topography of a great deal of
British folk-history: Avalon became the elysium of
King Arthur, Lyonnesse of King Mark. Tennyson's
*The Passing of Arthur* gives us the poetic quintessences
of the myth in these lines:

> A land of old unheaven from the abyss
> By fire to sink into the abyss again;
> Where fragments of forgotten people dwelt
> And the long mountains ended in a coast
> Of ever-shifting sand, and far away
> The phantom circle of a moaning sea. . . .
> So all day long the noise of battle roll'd
> Among the mountains by the winter sea,
> Until King Arthur's table, man by man,
> Had fall'n in Lyonnesse about their lord,
> King Arthur.

And so the last Romano-British king, having fallen
in battle against the barbarian invaders, is carried off
in his funeral barge to Avalon, the island valley

> Where falls not hail, or rain, or any snow,
> Nor ever wind blows loudly, but it lies
> Deep-meadow'd, happy, fair with orchard lawns
> And bowery hollows crown'd with summer seas.

It is, perhaps, appropriate to end this survey with a
poet's description of a lost land, since lands, like myths,
often vanish when the mystery, which was once so
much a part of intellectual life, is replaced by a purely
mechanistic view of the world. The modern scientist

and the medieval visionary are, admittedly, strange bedfellows. So, too, are the academic historian and the myth-maker. Certainly during the period of scepticism which was so typical of the late 19th-century scholarship, practically all myths were automatically discredited as fairy stories. The Deluge of the Bible, like the Atlantis of Plato, are examples. Today, discerning historians are not so sure.

The change of view has come about because the more we know about the twilight zones of early history, the more we realize that the folk-memory is a repository of otherwise unrecorded, or confusingly recorded, events. The legend of the Garden of Eden at one extreme and that of Lyonnesse at the other are cases in point, and science itself has come round to the view that there is more in these fables than it was formerly prepared to admit.

And so one always comes back to the first and greatest of these fables, since the man who gave it to us was a scholar of the highest intelligence and a philosopher of unquestioned integrity. Plato was honestly reporting an event which was, of course, as obscured by the mists of time as the story of King Arthur of Britain is to scholars today. He was, in other words, reconstructing the fall of an ancient empire in terms of a myth. And myths, as the Greek scientist Strabo pointed out, always have a kernel of truth. And more than that, perhaps, they are always concerned with some secret of civilization, or some significant relationship with a divine power, which we would be unwise to discredit or ignore.

# Appendix

THE following are the passages, in condensed form, from the two dialogues of Plato, the *Timaeus* and *Critias*, which give the gist of the Atlantis story:

Then listen, Socrates, to a tale which, though strange, is certainly true, having been attested by Solon, who was the wisest of the seven sages. He was a relative and a dear friend of my great-grandfather, Dropides; and he told the story to Critias, my grandfather, who remembered and repeated it to us. . . .

In the Egyptian Delta, at the head of which the river Nile divides, there is a certain district which is called the district of Sais, and the great city of the district is also called Sais. To this city came Solon, and was received there with great honour; he asked the priests who were most skilful in such matters, about antiquity, and made the discovery that neither he nor any other Hellene knew anything worth mentioning about the times of old.

(After some discussion concerning the mythological founding of Athens, Critias tells the story of Atlantis to Socrates. He claims to be speaking from memory and from Solon's notebooks.)

Let me begin by observing first of all, that nine thousand was the sum of years which had elapsed since the war which was said to have taken place between those who dwelt outside the Pillars of Heracles and all who dwelt within them; this war I am going to describe. Of the combatants on the one side, the city of Athens was reported to have been the leader and to have fought out the war; the combatants on the other side were commanded by the kings of Atlantis, which, as I have said, once existed, greater in extent than Libya and Asia, and afterwards when sunk by earthquake, became an impassable barrier of mud to those voyagers from hence who attempt to cross the ocean which lies beyond. . . .

Now Atlas had a numerous and honourable family, and they retained the kingdom, the eldest son handing it on to his eldest for many generations; and they had such an amount of wealth as was never before possessed by kings and potentates, and is not likely ever to be again, and they were furnished with everything which they needed, both in the city and country. For because of the greatness of their empire many things were brought to them from foreign countries, and the island itself provided most of what was required by them for the uses of life. In the first place, they dug out of the earth whatever was to be found there, solid as well as fusile, and that which is now only a name and was then something more than a name, orichalcum, was dug out of the earth in many parts of the island, being more precious in those days than anything except gold. There was an abundance of wood for carpenters' work, and sufficient maintenance for tame and wild animals. Moreover, there were a great number of elephants in the island; for as there was provision for all sorts of animals both for those which live in lakes and marshes and rivers, and also for those which live in mountains and on plains, so there was for the animal which is the largest and most voracious of all. Also whatever fragrant things there now are in the earth, whether roots or herbage, or woods, or essences which distil from fruit and flower, grew and thrived in that land; also the fruit which admits cultivation, both the dry sort, which is given us for nourishment, and any other which we use for food – we call them all by the common name of pulse, and the fruits having a hard rind, affording drinks and meats and ointments, and good store of chestnuts and the like, which furnish pleasure and amusement, and are fruits which spoil with keeping, and the pleasant kinds of dessert, with which we console ourselves after dinner, when we are tired of eating – all these that sacred island which then beheld the light of the sun, brought forth fair and wondrous and in infinite abundance. With such blessings the earth freely furnished them; meanwhile they went on constructing their temples and palaces and harbours and docks. And they arranged the whole country in the following manner:

First of all they bridged over the zones of sea which surrounded the ancient metropolis, making a road to and from the royal palace. And at the very beginning they built the palace in the habitation of the god and of their ancestors, which they continued to ornament in successive generations, every king surpassing the one who went before him to the utmost of his power, until they made the building a marvel to behold for size and for beauty. . . . The stone which was used in the work they quarried from underneath the centre island, and from underneath the zones, on the outer as well as the inner side. One kind was white, another black, and a third red, and as they quarried, they at the same time hollowed out docks double within, having roofs formed out of the native rock. Some of their buildings were simple, but in others they put together different stones, varying the colour to please the eye, and to be a natural source of delight. The entire circuit of the wall, which went round the outermost zone, they covered with a coating of brass, and the circuit of the next wall they coated with tin, and the third, which encompassed the citadel, flashed with the red light of orichalchum.

The palaces in the interior of the citadel were constructed on this wise: In the centre was a holy temple dedicated to Cleito and Poseidon, which remained inaccessible, and was surrounded by an enclosure of gold; this was the spot where the family of the ten princes was conceived and saw the light, and thither the people annually brought the fruits of the earth in their season from all the ten portions, to be an offering to each of the ten. Here was Poseidon's own temple which was a stadium in length, and half a stadium in width, and of a proportionate height having a strange barbaric appearance. All the outside of the temple, with the exception of the pinnacles, they covered with silver, and the pinnacles with gold. In the interior of the temple the roof was of ivory, curiously wrought everywhere with gold and silver and orichalcum; and all the other parts, the walls and pillars and floor, they coated with orichalcum. In the temple they placed statues of gold: there was the god himself standing in a chariot – the charioteer of six winged horses – and of such a size that he touched the roof of the building with his head; around him there were a hundred Nereides riding on dolphins, for such was thought to be the number of them by the men of those days. There were also in the interior of the temple other images which had been dedicated by private persons. And around the temple on the outside were placed statues of gold of all who had been numbered among the ten kings, both them and their wives, and there were many other great offerings of kings and of private persons, coming both from the city itself and from the foreign cities over which they held sway. There was an altar too, which in size and workmanship corresponded to this magnificence, and the palaces, in like manner, answered to the greatness of the kingdom and the glory of the temple.

In the next place, they had fountains, one of gold and another of hot water, in gracious plenty flowing; and they were wonderfully adapted for one by reason of the pleasantness and excellence of their waters. They constructed buildings about them and planted suitable trees; also they made cisterns, some open to the heaven, others roofed over, to be used in winter as warm baths; there were the kings' baths, and the baths of private persons, which were kept apart; and there were separate baths for women, and for horses and cattle, and to each of them they gave as much adornment as was suitable. . . .

Each of the ten kings in his own division and in his own city had the absolute control of the citizens, and, in most cases, of the laws, punishing and slaying whomsoever he would. Now the order of precedence among them and their mutual relations were regulated by the commands of Poseidon which the laws had handed down. These were inscribed by the first kings on a pillar of orichalchum, which was situated in the middle of the island, at the temple of Poseidon, whither the kings were gathered together every fifth year and every sixth year alternatively, thus giving equal honour to the odd and to the even number. And when they were gathered together they consulted about their common interests, and enquired if anyone had transgressed in anything, and passed judgment, and before they passed judgment, they gave their pledges to one another on this wise: There were bulls who had the range of the temple of Poseidon; and the ten kings, being left alone in the temple, after they had offered prayers to the god that they might capture the victim which was acceptable to him, hunted the bulls, without weapons, but with staves and nooses; and the bull which they caught they led up to the pillar and cut its throat over the top of it so that the blood fell upon the sacred inscription. Now on the pillar, besides the laws, there was inscribed an oath invoking mighty curses on the disobedient. When therefore, after slaying the bull in the accustomed manner, they proceeded to burn its limbs, they filled a bowl of wine and cast in a clot of blood for each of them; the rest of the victim they put in the fire, after having purified the column all round. Then they drew from the bowl in golden cups, and pouring a libation on the fire, they swore that they would judge according to the laws on the pillar, and would punish him who in any point had already transgressed them, and that for the future they would not, if they could help, offend against the writing on the pillar, and would neither command others, nor obey any ruler who commanded them, to act otherwise than according to the laws of their father Poseidon. This was the prayer which each of them offered up for himself and for his descendants, at the same time drinking and dedicating the cup out of which he drank in the temple of the god; and after they had supped and satisfied their needs, when darkness came on, and the fire about the sacrifice was cool, all of them put on most beautiful azure robes, and, sitting on the ground, at night over the embers of the sacrifices by which they had sworn, and extinguishing all the fire about the temple they received and gave judgment, if any of them had an accusation to bring against any one; and when they had given judgment, at daybreak they wrote down their sentences on a golden tablet, and dedicated it together with their robes to be a memorial.

There were many special laws affecting the several kings inscribed about the temples; but the most important was the following: They were not to take up arms against one another, and they were all to come to the rescue if anyone in any of their cities attempted to overthrow the royal house; like their ancestors, they were to deliberate in common about war and other matters, giving the supremacy to the descendants of Atlas. And the king was not to have the power of life and death over any of his kinsmen unless he had the assent of the majority of the ten.

Such was the vast power which the god settled in the lost island of Atlantis; and this he afterwards directed against our land for the following reasons, as tradition tells: For many generations, as long as the divine nature lasted in them, they were obedient to the laws, and well-affectioned towards the god, whose seed they were, for they possessed true and in every way great spirits, uniting gentleness with wisdom in the various chances of life, and in their intercourse with one another. They despised everything but virtue, caring little for their present state of life, and thinking lightly of the possession of gold and other property, which seemed only a burden to them; neither were they intoxicated by luxury; nor did wealth deprive them of their self-control; but they were sober, and saw clearly that all these goods are increased by virtue and friendship with one another, whereas by too great regard and respect for them they are lost, and virtue with them.

By such reflections and by the continuance in them of a divine nature, the qualities which we have described grew and increased among them; but when the divine portion began to fade slowly, and became diluted too often and too much with the mortal admixture, and the human nature got the upper hand, they then, being unable to bear their fortune, behaved unseemly, and to him who had an eye to see grew visibly debased, for they were losing the fairest of their precious gifts; but to those who had no eye to see the true happiness, they appeared glorious and blessed at the very time when they were becoming tainted with unrighteous ambition and power. Zeus, the god of gods, who rules according to law, and is able to see into such things, perceiving that an honourable race was in a woeful plight, and wanting to inflict punishment on them that they might be chastened and improve, collected all the gods into their most holy habitation, which, being placed in the centre of the world, beholds all created things. And when he had called them together, he spake as follows:

At this point the unfinished *Critias* breaks off.

# Bibliography

THE following short list of books is recommended as a guide to further reading. Most of the titles given here also contain fairly comprehensive bibliographies which readers who wish to follow up some of the theories suggested in this survey may find useful.

H. S. Bellamy, *The Atlantis Myth*, 1948.

H. P. Blavatsky, *The Secret Doctrine*, 1888.

J. Bramwell, *Lost Atlantis*, 1938.

J. Churchward, *The Lost Continent of Mu*, 1959.
                 *The Sacred Symbols of Mu*, 1960.

I. Donnelly, *Atlantis: The Antediluvian World*, 1949.

W. A. Jones, *Blavatsky and Hoerbiger*, 1950.

A. Le Plongeon, *Queen Moo and the Egyptian Sphinx*, 1896.

J. B. Leslie, *Submerged Atlantis Restored*, 1911.

J. V. Luce, *The End of Atlantis*, 1970.

Plato, *Timaeus* and *Critias*, translated by B. Jowett.

W. Scott-Elliott, *The Story of Atlantis and the Lost Lemuria*, 1962.

V. Slessarev, *Prester John: The Letter and the Legend*, 1959.

J. Spanuth, *Atlantis: The Mystery Unravelled*, 1956.

J. L. T. C. Spence, *The History of Atlantis*, 1926.

*The Problem of Lemuria*, 1932.

R. Steiner, *Atlantis and Lemuria*, 1896.

J. F. Webb (translator), *The Voyage of St Brendan*, 1965.

E. M. Wishaw, *Atlantis in Andalusia*, 1929.

# Notes

1. *The Dialogues of Plato*, translated by B. Jowett, Vol. III, pp. 702–3 and 787.
2. *Critias*. Ibid., Vol. III, p. 803.
3. Notably Jürgen Spanuth in *Atlantis: The Mystery Unravelled*, 1956, p. 27.
4. There is no Troano Codex in the British Museum except, of course, the facsimile taken from the original, which is in the National Museum of Madrid.
5. Augustus Le Plongeon, MD, *Queen Moo and the Egyptian Sphinx*, 1896, p. xviii.
6. Ibid., p. xxiv.
7. Diego de Landa, *Relación de las cosas de Yucatan . . . 1556*, 1881, p. 47.
8. Le Plongeon, op. cit., p. 147.
9. Troano Codex, Part II, plates ii to v.
10. Rudbeck's *Atland eller Manheim* was first published in Swedish with a Latin translation at Upsala in 1679.
11. *Atlantis: The Mystery Unravelled.*
12. K. G. Zschaetzsch, *Atlantis: die Urheimet der Arier*, 1934.
13. Le Plongeon, op. cit., pp. 38 and 206–7.
14. Ignatius Donelly, *Atlantis: The Antediluvian World*, modern revised edition edited by Egerton Sykes, 1949, p. 1.
15. Ibid., foreword by Egerton Sykes, p. ix.
16. For a discussion of the tomb of Tin Hinan, see James Wellard's *The Great Sahara*, 1965, pp. 46–50.

17. Josef Karst, *Atlantis und der liby-äthiopische Kulturkeis*, 1931.

18. E. M. Wishaw, *Atlantis in Andalusia*, 1929.

19. *Atlantis: die Urheimet der Arier*.

20. *Atlantis: The Mystery Unravelled*.

21. W. Scott-Elliott, *The Story of Atlantis and the Lost Lemuria*, first published in 1896 and 1904, reprinted in 1930 and 1954, and re-issued by the Theosophical Press in 1962. 1962 edition, p. 88.

22. For a sample biography, see Lewis Spence, *The Problem of Lemuria*, 1932.

23. Helena Petrovna Blavatsky, *The Secret Doctrine*, 1888.

24. Rudolf Steiner, *Atlantis and Lemuria*, 1896.

25. *The Story of Atlantis and the Lost Lemuria*

26. Ibid., p. 92.

27. Ibid., p. 48.

28. Colonel James Churchward, *The Lost Continent of Mu*, 1959, p. 47.

29. Ibid., p. 51.

30. See his article, 'The Lost Continent', in *The Times*, 19 February 1909.

31. S. Marinatos, 'The Volcanic Destruction of Minoan Crete', *Antiquity*, Vol. 13, 1939, pp. 425–39.

32. *The Voyage of St Brendan*, translated by J. F. Webb, 1965, p. 59.

33. O. G. S. Crawford, 'Lyonnesse', *Antiquity*, Vol. 1, 1927, p. 5.